FAITH AND DOUBT TODAY

FAITH AND DOUBT TODAY

Personal Responses to Spiritual Struggles

Philip St. Romain

LIGUORI
PUBLICATIONS

One Liguori Drive
Liguori, Missouri 63057
(314) 464-2500

Imprimi Potest:
John F. Dowd, C.SS.R.
Provincial, St. Louis Province
Redemptorist Fathers

Imprimatur:
+ Edward J. O'Donnell
Vicar General, Archdiocese of St. Louis

ISBN 0-89243-245-4
Library of Congress Catalog Card Number: 85-82033

Copyright © 1985, Liguori Publications
Printed in U.S.A.

Cover design by Pam Hummelsheim

About the Author

Philip St. Romain is a popular author, lecturer, and retreat director. His background includes a Master's degree in biology, three years on a campus ministry team at Louisiana State University, and five years as a substance abuse prevention consultant for the Louisiana Department of Education.

Married and the father of two daughters, Mr. St. Romain resides in Baton Rouge, Louisiana. His several books include *Becoming a New Person, Catholic Answers to Fundamentalists' Questions,* and *How to Form a Christian Growth Support Group,* published by Liguori.

Currently, Philip St. Romain is the director of Personal Growth Services, Inc., a nonprofit organization that offers workshops, lectures, and retreats on a variety of topics. (For more information, write Personal Growth Services, Inc., 13586 Neil Avenue, Baton Rouge, LA 70810. Phone: 504/766-7615.)

Contents

Acknowledgments

This book is the result of my own struggle to grow in faith during a time in history when faith does not come easily. The four primary sources of doubt discussed in this book — namely selfishness, scientific materialism, the problem of suffering and evil, and secular humanism — have plagued me since my earliest days of adult faith. During the past eleven years, I have discovered that most Christians attempting to grow in faith must also come to grips with these four issues. This book represents an attempt to share what I have learned about faith and doubt from my own struggles and from the many Christian friends and writers who have helped me along the way.

John Sylvest and John Edmunds, S.T., have been helpful dialogue partners through the years, especially concerning the challenges of scientific materialism and the problem of human suffering. My dear friend, Herman Sensat, has taught me much about suffering as he continues in his battle against cancer. Lisa, my wife, and Rita and Theresa, my daughters, also deserve a special word for their ongoing support and encouragement, and for helping me through the years to become less selfish.

Finally, I would like to express my gratitude to Roger Marchand and the Liguori editorial staff for their practical suggestions and encouragement. Their resource suggestions have also been most helpful.

Introduction

A few years ago an elderly man expressed a few sentiments that I have never forgotten. We had been participating in an intensive encounter-type support group for about a week as part of a counselor-training course we were attending. The time had come for us to say our good-byes and summarize what the course had meant to us. "This has all been fine and good," the old man began, glancing around the room, "but I wish I could take something of the care I have found here and keep it growing."

"You will find this kind of care wherever you find people," replied the group facilitator, encouraging him.

"No, I won't!" objected the old man. "I've been on this earth too long to believe in that sort of dream any longer."

An uncomfortable silence settled in. Everyone was ready to go home, and here was this old man raising a new and significant issue. We could not drop it and leave him hanging there, but we all had hotels to check out of and planes to catch.

"Didn't you find care and acceptance from people during the past week?" queried the facilitator, hoping to restore the old man's faith in people.

"I did," he replied, "but it was somewhat superficial. After we all leave, the warm glow within us will quickly fade; we will soon forget about each other. It has been nice, but life is not a group encounter session. Most people do not give a damn about me nor about anyone else but themselves! I'm not any different," he lamented. "It's just that at my age, one becomes a little sick of it all. One hopes for more from life than a temporary kindness here and there."

"It sounds to me like what you're really asking for is faith in God," I interjected.

This "outlandish" proposition caused further discomfort among group members. The word *God* had not been mentioned all week, yet the entire thrust of our course had been directed toward facilitating human growth. Even so, it had been obvious from the start that most of the people in our group were agnostics or, at best, lapsed Christians.

The old man looked at me gratefully, however. "Young man," he said, "if I could bring myself to really believe in God, I would dance with joy through the rest of my years."

"Then why don't you believe in him?" replied the facilitator, as though faith were merely one of many human options — such as taking a nice trip or learning a new hobby.

"I've tried, but I don't get very far with it," the old man returned. "There's too much evil and pain in the world; and besides, there's no proof that he exists anyway. Science, after all, can explain the universe with no reference to God. It's just too hard to believe in him," he concluded.

"And yet something within you still cries out for God," I noted. "Why do you think that is?"

"I don't really know," he replied.

At this, the facilitator called upon the next participant to share her perceptions of the week. It was difficult to concentrate on what the others said, however, for the old man's pathos seemed to me the most authentic sentiment I had heard expressed that entire week.

I share this memory because in that single conversation we find summarized many of the kinds of struggles in faith that people are experiencing today. Faith has never been easy, but it is probably harder to come to in our modern world than at any time in history.

No longer do we live in a culture that encourages and supports faith. The so-called Christian culture that the Western world once enjoyed has been shattered and fragmented into various pluralistic options. In the absence of conventional support, personal faith has become a tremendous struggle. As the old man rightly stated, there are many reasons to doubt God's existence. Faith, if it is to be real, must therefore come to grips with the many kinds of doubts which assail the people of our day.

Faith and Doubt

"Now faith is the assurance of things hoped for, the conviction of things not seen," wrote the author of the Letter to the Hebrews (11:1). Notice in this classical definition the relationship between faith and hope: faith is the assurance that what we hope for shall come to pass. Since this definition is concerned with "things not seen," or spiritual reality, faith is the assurance that our spiritual hopes shall be fulfilled — that we shall come to know and love God.

Doubt may be defined as any obstacle that makes faith difficult or that even moves us away from faith altogether. In its extreme manifestation it becomes despair, the conviction that human hopes cannot be fulfilled at all. On an emotional level, doubt leads to insecurity and guilt.

Because we are spiritual as well as physical and psychological in nature, there is a part of us that longs for God and can be fulfilled only by God. Faith is the bridge which establishes relationship between a person and God. Doubt assails the bridge as well as belief in the God who builds the bridge.

But why doubt at all? If it is indeed true that there is God and that we are capable of knowing and being known by God through faith, then why should we ever doubt either God's existence or his goodness? Part of the answer to this is, surely, that our knowing through faith is imperfect. We must also consider the fact that our relationship with God changes as we get older and become more mature. Knowledge and experience change the way we view ourselves and reality. These changes can create a tension that affects our human relationships as well as our relationship with God. Because we change, our approach to God has to grow through the years. "When I was a child, I spoke like a child, I thought like a child, I reasoned like a child; when I became a man, I gave up childish ways," wrote Saint Paul (1 Corinthians 13:11). Childish faith cannot support adult experiences. Unfortunately, many of us have failed to grow in our relationship with God as we have grown in our knowledge of business, politics, or other more worldly concerns. Doubt, for such people, is the natural consequence of spiritual neglect.

Still, there is even more to the phenomenon of doubt than simply an imperfect knowledge of God and a failure to grow. Even the greatest of saints have struggled with doubt, and it is certain that they did not suffer from spiritual neglect. Through the course of this book we shall refer to Evil Spirit as a force that opposes the coming of God's Kingdom by leading us to sin. Since doubt gnaws away at our relationship with God, Evil Spirit utilizes doubt as a means to cut people off from grace and, consequently, to move them toward a life of selfishness. I am not saying that all of our doubts about God are thoughts introduced by Satan; most of our uncertainties concerning the reality of God and his ways are natural and sincere. But it is the work of Evil Spirit to twist and distort our natural doubts to such an extent that they lead us away from the kind of intimacy with God that furthers his work among humankind.

There are many specific kinds of doubts which assail faith, and it would be impossible to address them all in one short book. Doubt, like faith, assumes as many unique manifestations as there are individuals. Something that causes one individual to doubt may be no problem at all to another. I have found this to be true even in my own marriage; issues that have caused me deep anguish do not even ruffle my wife, and conversely so. (This, by the way, points up the value of sharing our doubts with others and leaning on their faith when we need to.) Nevertheless, I believe it is possible to identify four basic issues that bring some measure of doubt into the lives of millions of people today:

1. *Selfishness,* which moves us away from relationships with God and others and cuts us off from spiritual power. Consumerism, hedonism, and narcissism are common avenues to selfishness.

2. *Scientific materialism,* an intellectual form of doubt which claims that we live in a universe devoid of ultimate purpose and meaning, and which claims that faith is an irrational absurdity.

3. *Suffering and evil,* which lead us to ask: Why is there so much pain in this world if there really is a good and powerful God?

4. *Secular humanism,* which implies that faith in God is irrelevant to furthering peace, prosperity, and justice in this world.

We are all affected by these four common sources of doubt in our modern world. Like invisible demons, they each insidiously diminish our capacity for cultivating a deep and abiding faith in God's unconditional love for us. They are part of the spiritual atmosphere of the twentieth century. They creep into our schools, media, and even into the Church. But as the great saints and movers of history have taught us, it is entirely possible to cultivate a strong faith even in the face of overwhelming doubts. Faith can never eliminate doubt, but it can certainly outflank it and become a primary force in our lives. In order for it to do so, however, we must face our doubts squarely and call them by name so they can be "exorcised." We cannot grow in faith by ignoring our doubts nor,

15

especially, by running away from them. Faith, if it is to be real, must overcome doubt by working through it. That is what this book will attempt to assist in.

About This Book

Each of the four sources of doubt — selfishness, scientific materialism, evil, and secular humanism — can raise very complex questions to which simplistic answers are not satisfactory. Selfishness, for example, is often not terribly different from self-love. Scientific materialism negates God, but it has helped us to advance our understanding of the cosmos. What sometimes appears to us to be evil may, in the long run, produce great good. And there can be no doubt that the world is a better place because of the work done by many secular humanists. I shall therefore try to avoid splitting semantical hairs when discussing these issues. My real concern is faith and doubt, and my reflections will attempt to keep this focus throughout. This means that I will critique these four sources of doubt only insofar as they impact and erode religious faith. Additional discussion regarding the wider implications of these issues is recommended at the end of the book in the section "Suggested Reading."

Some readers might be more interested in certain chapters but not others, so let me mention here that each chapter is fairly self-contained. Although there is a continuity in thematic development from one chapter to the next, there will be nothing lost by skipping chapters or reading them out of sequence. I would challenge readers, however, to avoid underestimating the manner in which even so familiar a force as selfishness erodes religious faith. In fact, scientific materialism, secular humanism, and other kinds of doubts lead us away from God precisely because they leave us to ourselves alone.

Chapter 5, "The Response of Faith," will move us beyond a mere response to sources of doubt toward a positive spiritual orientation. How do we "get" the assurance and conviction of things hoped for that the author of Hebrews encourages us to embrace? That shall be our topic in Chapter 5. Faith, after all, must ultimately achieve its focus in God and not simply away from doubt. When it is deeply centered in God, faith renders many doubts inconsequential. Chapter 5 will attempt to help us toward a fuller experience of life in the Holy Spirit.

The questions for Reflection/Discussion at the end of each chapter are intended to help one reflect on the manner in which faith and doubt interact in one's life. It may be helpful to use a journal to respond to these questions; that way they can be examined again later. Also, I believe sharing responses in a discussion group would be a powerful experience. We all struggle with the kinds of issues raised in this book, and we need each other for support and understanding if we are to persevere in faith.

The Challenge
of Selfishness

> A man's being is his potential energy directed towards
> or away from God: and it is by this potential energy that
> he will be judged as good or evil — for it is possible, in
> the language of the Gospel, to commit adultery and
> murder in the heart, even while remaining blameless in
> action. (Aldous Huxley, *The Perennial Philosophy*)

Mr. Smith works over fifty hours a week so that his family can
enjoy the better things in life. He spends little time with his wife
and children; the children do not know him very well. Yet, his wife
maintains that Mr. Smith is a loving father — why else would he
work so hard to give them so many nice things? Is Mr. Smith
selfish? Is his wife selfish?

Mrs. Buford spends her days taking care of her two toddlers and
keeping the books for her husband's small business. After several
days with no break, she decides to call a sitter to care for the
children while she spends an evening out with a friend. Is she being
selfish?

Mr. Crawford is retired and lives alone. He seldom gets out of
the house, even though he is in excellent health. When family
members visit, he is cordial but cool. His general life stance seems

to be, "Leave me alone, and I'll leave you alone." Is this selfishness?

I know people who would state that the individuals in the above cases are all acting selfishly. Mr. Smith, they would say, is probably copping out of relationships with his wife and children and is masking it with a materialistic notion of love. They would also say that Mrs. Buford is probably running away from her household duties, although it's surely no great sin to get out once in awhile. As for Mr. Crawford, he's obviously a crank; he cares little about the welfare of others, so he is selfish.

Other people could defend each of the individuals as acting unselfishly — even out of great love! Mr. Smith, for example, might really be doing the best he can to love his family. Mrs. Buford, in taking time to love herself, is recharging her spiritual batteries for the sake of her family. The reclusive Mr. Crawford is not hurting anyone, nor is he seeking anything from anyone; thus he is not selfish.

We all know people like Mr. Smith, Mrs. Buford, and Mr. Crawford. We all have sought to understand the morality of their behavior, using the kinds of arguments discussed above. Their lives, you see, are much like our own. And we all certainly wonder about our own lives — whether we are good people, doing what is right.

Part of the difficulty in discernment can undoubtedly be traced to a lack of clarity concerning the difference between selfishness and self-love. Our training has taught us to regard selfishness as wrong but self-love as appropriate. But what's the difference? Indeed, is there a difference?

Selfishness and Self-Love

It is unfortunate that the classical literature in Christian spirituality has used the term self-love to refer to what, I believe, is really selfishness. Time and again *The Imitation of Christ* adjures us to turn away from self-love. And the Gospels themselves state that the first step in following Christ must be self-denial (Mark 8:34). Many Christians have correctly understood that these readings were not intended to justify putting ourselves down, but I am afraid that in far too many cases that is precisely what happened. We mistakenly interpreted the spiritual writings' condemnations of selfishness as a condemnation of self-love, thus denying ourselves the basic self-acceptance that is a prerequisite to real loving.

Perhaps it was the inability to formulate a theology of self-love that brought about the narcissism of the 1960s and 1970s. Consider, for example, a quote from philosopher Ayn Rand's provocative little book *The Virtue of Selfishness:*

> In popular usage, the word ''selfishness'' is a synonym of evil; the image it conjures is of a murderous brute who tramples over piles of corpses to achieve his own ends, who cares for no living being and pursues nothing but the gratification of the mindless whims of any immediate moment.
>
> Yet the exact meaning and dictionary definition of the word ''selfishness'' is: concern with one's own interests.

Rand goes on in her classical novels and essays to formulate an ethical philosophy based on rational self-interest. Respect for freedom and mutual agreements characterize her vision and the vision of other contemporary self-help writers. Their message emphatically encourages us to accept ourselves, to forgive ourselves, to have fun, to do what we would like without seeking permission from others, etc. Although this kind of ''me-centeredness'' is not without its ethical pitfalls, I believe it has brought a healing kind of liberation to people who were living under great psychological and spiritual oppression.

Perhaps a quote from Saint Augustine can clarify the classical usage of the term *self-love:*

> The city of God is made by the love of God pushed to the contempt of self; the earthly city, by the love of self pushed to the contempt of God.

I believe this is precisely what the spiritual writers of the ages really meant when they denounced self-love. I believe, too, that this is what most of us think about when we use the term *selfishness.*

Even though Ayn Rand's definition (which is also Webster's) suggests nothing that is contemptuous of God, let us for semantical purposes define selfishness as *self-interest that is contemptuous of the needs of others and is, therefore, contemptuous of God.* The Buddhists call it *Tanha,* egocentric striving, and they maintain that such selfishness is at the root of all human suffering. It consists of all those "inclinations which tend to continue or increase separateness, the separate existence of the subject of desire. . . . " (Christmas Humphreys, *Buddhism*).

Self-love, on the other hand, refers to a kind of self-interest that enables us to grow in relationship with others. The example of Mrs. Buford at the beginning of this chapter might be a case in point. Doing what is necessary to keep ourselves alive and growing in order to enrich our relationships is what self-love is all about. Most of us could stand to grow more fully in this area.

The essential difference between selfishness and self-love, then, lies in its orientation toward God and others. Accordingly, it may at times be difficult to judge whether a person's behavior is selfish or self-loving. That is why Jesus told us not to judge other people (although he did not say that we should ignore evil); in judging others, we are really projecting our own motives for behavior onto them (thus judging ourselves). Discerning selfishness and self-love in our motives is a necessary but tricky discipline, for the appearance of selfishness in our motives is often insidious and difficult to recognize.

For example, if I go to a professional workshop to enhance my counseling skills for my own growth and for the sake of my patients, that is self-loving. But if I go to enhance my résumé for the sake of professional status, that may be selfish. Quite obviously, then, many of our actions are rooted in a combination of both selfishness and self-love. Both wheat and darnel sprout in our motives (see Matthew 13:24-30), and it would be a great mistake to postpone action until our motives are completely pure.

I, for my part, can state that I have never had a completely pure motive. Writing this book, for example, is in part an attempt to clarify my own thinking while catalyzing growth in others. Surely, too, there is a hope for money and recognition mixed into my motives. Like the tenants in Jesus' parable of the wheat and weeds, the best we can do is to allow selfishness and self-love to coexist in our souls and to remain ever alert to the ripening of selfishness. We need to be alert so that we can separate the weeds from the wheat and burn them in the fires of repentance. We must be careful not to kill self-love in our efforts to avoid selfishness. Achieving this balance requires reflection, mortification, and God's grace. Without such discipline the seeds of selfishness, I am convinced, will prevail over self-love, corrupting our souls while producing great evil in our lives.

Manifestations of Selfishness

Questions concerning how selfishness manifests itself in our lives naturally come to the fore now. In my book *Becoming a New Person* (Liguori, 1984) I spoke of selfishness as a distortion of our legitimate quests for pleasure, esteem, and security. These three forms of selfishness are distinct, but they often reinforce one another. Let us focus on them by reflecting on the three temptations of Christ in Matthew 4:1-11. As Father John Powell has pointed out, the three temptations of Jesus were invitations to pursue pleasure, esteem, and security for selfish purposes.

1. Pleasure. In the first temptation, the devil invites a starving Jesus to turn stones into bread. Bread is the end product of a long series of labors, from cultivating and planting to milling and baking. So, in effect, this temptation was an enticement to bypass human effort to meet physical needs. Pleasure is the emotional gratification experienced when physical needs are met. What the devil was really asking Jesus to do was to seek pleasure without working for it.

In our own lives, this temptation invites us to make the will-to-pleasure the primary motive for our behavior. If we fall prey to this trap, we become selfish; for, as Jesus noted,

> Man shall not live by bread alone,
> but by every word that proceeds from
> the mouth of God. (Matthew 4:4)

In its extreme manifestations this striving to live by bread alone takes the forms of gluttony and lust. It is sanctioned by the philosophies of rational hedonism, better known as consumerism or materialism, which promise to deliver happiness through self-indulgence and possessions. Because they are contemptuous of the needs of others, gluttony and lust are manifestations of selfishness in our lives.

2. Esteem. The devil promised to make Jesus the king of the world if only Jesus would do the devil homage (Matthew 4:8-9). This is a case in which the will-to-esteem is pushed to its ultimate manifestation, the will-to-power. Our psychological need to be loved and esteemed by others is very legitimate. But it, too, can become perverted — as, indeed, the devil would have it. One common perversion is narcissism, or pride. Pride, here, does not mean the feeling we experience when we do a job well. It means the kind of vanity that makes the ego its own point of justification. Arrogance, condescension, and snobbery result from the will-to-esteem gone awry. The pursuit of social status (''keeping up with the Joneses'') is another form of it, which naturally leads to prejudice against ''inferiors.'' That is why Jesus rejected this temptation, saying that it is not the self nor the devil that must be worshiped, but the Lord God alone (Matthew 4:10).

3. Security. '' . . . throw yourself down; for it is written, 'He will give his angels charge of you,' '' tempted the devil (see Matthew 4:5-6). The will-to-security, when it becomes selfish, seeks something similar. We all need a certain amount of security if we are to function well in this world, but in its selfish manifestations the will-to-security is one of the most destructive of human drives.

Those who actively pursue security usually become controlling, greedy, and manipulative. The rich man in the Gospels tried to lay up goods in his bins so he would never again have to work (Luke 12:16-21). Like that man, the idolaters of security also strive to guarantee their future well-being. This striving produces avarice and envy, two very destructive manifestations of selfishness.

Others seek security by passively abandoning themselves and their needs into the care of others. This is laziness. Surely, it is much harder to climb down from a temple top than it is to jump down and wait for the angels to cushion life's blows; similarly, it is much easier to withdraw from life and to let others take care of us than to persist in the ongoing struggle to grow as human beings by working to meet our needs. ''You shall not tempt the Lord your God'' by this kind of abandonment, said Jesus (see Matthew 4:7).

The three temptations to selfishness present themselves to us daily. They are promoted through our media in the guise of rational self-interest. But they quickly deteriorate into hedonism, narcissism, and laziness if they are not submitted to a higher, balancing principle. We see these manifestations of selfishness in our own lives, in our families and communities, and even in nations. Some of the greatest evils in history have come about when governments have supported their peoples' hedonism by exploiting others — or when they have asserted their narcissistic pride by persecuting "inferior" people — or when they have gambled on security by piling up food and weapons. As we shall see shortly, selfishness in its social manifestations is a powerful source of doubt in today's world. It also serves the interests of evil, which is another source of doubt.

The Origins of Selfishness

Selfishness, as we have noted, is a perversion of our legitimate strivings for pleasure, esteem, and security. So it is only natural to ask: Why do these motives become perverted in the first place — especially if we pay such negative consequences because of selfishness? Why don't we just do away with selfishness and become people who recognize our interdependence? Why not indeed!

In trying to respond to these questions, we shall see how selfishness pervades our world and how it perpetuates itself in generation after generation. The biological and cultural origins of selfishness explain much; they point to the beginning of a way out of the problem. Nevertheless, there is much about selfishness that remains a mystery.

First of all, selfishness is rooted in our individual instinct for self-preservation. All animals are genetically programmed to do what is necessary to keep the body alive, at least long enough to reproduce. We human beings are no different in this respect. There is no longer any doubt that at our unconscious levels we, too, possess sexual and aggressive drives. This innate selfishness shows up most clearly in small children; they want what they want when they want it, without considering the needs of their parents or anyone else. We come into the world as selfish animals. It is the role of cultural wisdom to temper those instincts and channel them in appropriate directions.

This brings us to a *second* consideration: the influence of the human environment or culture. Parents who model selfish behaviors deprive their children of the skills they need to learn in order to live unselfishly. Jesus took this matter very seriously, warning us that ". . . whoever causes one of these little ones who believe in me to sin, it would be better for him to have a great millstone fastened round his neck and to be drowned in the depth of the sea." (Matthew 18:6) Cultural ignorance and superstitions are other examples, as are messages that promote hedonism, narcissism, and an unhealthy striving for security.

The *third* source of selfish behavior is physical and mental illnesses. Some of the madmen of history have been mentally ill or plagued by diseases, such as syphilis, and tumors that destroy brain tissue and make it difficult to exercise responsible judgment. Alcoholism and drug addiction are other cases in point. Even though these maladies are in part self-inflicted, there is no doubt that the addict loses the ability to make responsible decisions while under the influence of mood-altering chemicals.

A *fourth* source of selfish behavior is stress. It is not so much that stress is self-oriented but that it so quickly erodes any disciplines we might have cultivated to counter selfish drives or environmental temptations. Hunger, anger, loneliness, and tiredness (H.A.L.T. — to use an acronym popular in self-help programs) all produce stress within us. They tie up huge reserves of psychic energy and wear down our resistance to self-destructive behavior. This is certainly true in my own life; when I am tired, for example, I am less kind and patient than when I am rested. One of the most loving things I can do during such times is to take a short nap. Tragically, single parents with small children do not have this luxury when they are tired; their children often suffer the consequences (as do children from all families when parents are tired, to be sure). Author M. Scott Peck, in his provocative book *People of the Lie,* points out that tiredness stress was partly responsible for blunting the moral consciences of the soldiers who participated in the My Lai massacre.

Because of the fast pace of living so many of us experience, and because we are so poor at practicing stress-management techniques, stress is a major killer today. It has been implicated in heart disease, cancer, ulcers, depression, child abuse, alcoholism, and other common maladies. It destroys bodies and, perhaps more seriously, wrecks relationships.

A *fifth* source of selfishness is more difficult to substantiate, but it is nonetheless real. Religious teachers through the ages have called it sin. Sin is a power that works through the above sources, using them to twist our noblest strivings into self-seeking motives. "For I do not do the good I want, but the evil I do not want is what I do," wrote Saint Paul, describing this mystery. "Now if I do what I do not want, it is no longer I that do it, but sin which dwells within me." (Romans 7:19-20)

Those who do not value religious teaching will debate this point; they will maintain that the instincts, cultural influences, physical and mental illnesses, and stress are adequate explanations of selfish behavior. Their arguments are difficult to counter because the mystery of sin is such that it does not admit of such direct observation as do the other sources of selfishness. But the insight of the religious is that *it is precisely because of the power of sin that our instincts for self-preservation, our cultural influences, our illnesses and stressful attitudes so quickly degenerate into destructiveness.*

In all selfishness there is an element of rebelliousness against what is good and true and necessary for our survival. This element of selfishness cannot be explained in terms of mere ignorance or instinct. Christianity has identified this source of rebelliousness as Satan, a spiritual being who has turned against God and is now attempting to influence others away from God. It is much more difficult to substantiate the influence of Satan and its army of demons than it is, say, the influence of the instincts or of consumerism (although cases of demonic possession have been studied seriously of late; see Malachi Martin's book *Hostage to the Devil*). Does this mean that all selfish people are possessed by the devil? Of course not! The devil has no need to possess the rigidly selfish, for they are already doing its will.

Self-preserving instincts, cultural influences, illnesses, and stress are means through which the power of sin causes a perversion of the will-to-pleasure, the will-to-esteem, and the will-to-security. Sin twists these strivings, turning them away from God and the well-being of ourselves and others. It causes us, like Saint Paul, to doubt whether our deepest hopes can be fulfilled. "Wretched man that I am!" we must all say if we are the least bit reflective. "Who will deliver me from this body of death?" (Romans 7:24) This is the doubt of a man who recognizes the futility of trying to find happiness through selfish means. Happily, Paul then goes on to describe the key role of faith in plugging us into the spiritual power necessary to overcome the forces of sin in the world.

Stages of Selfishness

In the Introduction to this book we defined doubt as a movement away from faith and hope. And in this chapter we have been reflecting on the manifestations and sources of human selfishness. Now it is time to examine the relationships between selfishness and doubt.

I believe selfishness to be the most common cause of religious doubt in today's world. Indeed, the other three causes of doubt that are discussed in the following chapters are destructive precisely because they lead to human selfishness. These causes are messages from the environment that influence the way we understand our drives for self-preservation, our world, and our place in the world. If these causes did not lead to an increase in selfishness, they probably would have no significant impact on religious doubt. This essential connection between selfishness and religious doubt is the reason we are studying human selfishness from several different angles.

First of all, let us admit that all people are selfish. We all, at some time in our lives, seek our will in contempt of God's will. Indeed, it is in the nature of selfishness not even to consider what God's will might be.

In his little classic *Lift Up Your Heart,* Bishop Fulton Sheen devoted considerable reflection to analyzing the psychology of egotism. He described several stages of selfishness, ranging from anticipation to habituation. These stages, of course, are not like separate compartments; they are merely helpful divisions of a reality that has differing degrees. All of us have experienced selfishness, but some of us are more selfish than others. The four stages of selfishness described below are an adaptation of Bishop Sheen's stages. They are also similar to one of the models of chemical dependency prevailing in the field of substance abuse counseling.

The **first stage** represents *anticipation*. The person considers the selfish behavior and makes a commitment ''in the heart'' to pursue it when circumstances permit. Plotting revenge, lusting after someone, coveting goods, and daydreaming about how to impress others are common examples. God is not yet spurned, although the will is beginning to move away from him.

The **second stage** consists of *experimental indulgences*. Not yet willing to let our hair get wet in the waters of selfishness, we indulge ourselves only occasionally. We overeat and overdrink, but only "on special occasions." Our efforts at status are not sustained, but we do not miss an opportunity to "advance ourselves socially." We do not measure ourselves against the Joneses, but neither do we "pass up a good bargain," even if it means living above our financial means. We pursue the extramarital affair, but state that "it's nothing serious — really!" We still experience sufficient freedom to find God, but at this stage we are becoming increasingly contemptuous of God's will. Thoughts of God bring us face-to-face with our guilt and shame, and we would rather not look at that. Besides, we're having a pretty good time at this stage and don't want a party pooper like God intruding.

The **third stage** is *habituation,* and here is where the fun begins to wane. Undisciplined by higher principles, the will spontaneously begins the selfish pursuit of pleasure, security, esteem, and power. Getting high on alcohol is not the exception but the rule. The sexual rendezvous is not a carefully planned adventure but a normal occurrence. Status seekers are working harder than ever on "advancing." Monetary securities are being accumulated for avaricious rather than prudent reasons. Because self-indulgent ends justify whatever means are necessary, behavior often conflicts with values. At this stage, people might still be found in churches; they may even be performing various liturgical functions or holding a place on the parish council — especially if these activities contribute to a sense of social status. But guilt and shame are accumulating. Rationalizations and projections keep others from confronting successfully. God is "back burnered." Relationships dry up. The inner self cries out in loneliness, but it is neglected.

The **fourth stage** is what Bishop Sheen called *necessary indulgence.* It represents an almost complete loss of control over the selfish behavior. It is *addiction* to selfishness. What began in anticipation now controls one's life. What was once freely chosen in experimentation now does the choosing for us. Even though this addiction might be to only one "small" indulgence, its erosion of the will is sufficient to undermine the whole personality. Thus the alcoholic, who otherwise is a fine spouse and worker, now faces a deterioration of his marriage and job. The social climber at this stage does not hesitate to trample upon others who are in her way. The security seeker cannot pile up enough money — and so forth. Reinforced by strong rationalizing defenses (learned so well in Stage Two), the addict projects his or her personality deficiencies onto others, and blames them for personal failures. Great evil can happen through these people, especially to their children.

People in Stage Four are extremely resistant to change. Even though their inner selves are in great spiritual and psychological distress, their defenses reinforce a perverted kind of pride that repulses others. Meanwhile, their wills go on functioning more or less out of control. Needless to say, these people have no interest in God's will, although they may continue to be found in and around churches and may even quote Scripture quite copiously. Their religious involvements are self-serving — makeshift attempts to keep others from believing that they are doing wrong. They are enshrouding their evil with a semblance of good so that others will admire them or at least not criticize them. This matter of living a lie is what prompted Scott Peck to label persons enmeshed in evil as "People of the Lie."

People in Stage Four are, for all practical purposes, atheists. As Bishop Sheen wrote in *Lift Up Your Heart,* "The new atheism is not of the intellect, but of the will; it is not an act of free and eager rejection of morality and its demands." Addicts of selfishness experience religious doubt, and lead others to doubt, because they do not want the light of God's truth shining on their evil hearts. "There is no man in the world who knows there is no God; but the modern atheist *wishes* there were no God," concluded Sheen.

At no time in this chapter have we spoken of selfish behavior as intentional or unintentional. This omission has not been accidental. No one of us can tell whether another person is intentionally or involuntarily selfish, and I do not believe it matters very much; the damage is about the same either way. For example, my training as a biologist and substance abuse counselor has convinced me that alcoholism and certain mental illnesses are the result of genetic predispositions that we cannot control. I am therefore quite willing to concede that most alcoholics do not set out to become addicted to alcohol. I am even willing to say that most of the selfish behavior that accompanies alcoholism is probably not intended. This can help us to avoid passing moral judgment on the *intentions* of alcoholics as well as others who have been set up by Nature or the environment (abused children) to fall into the snares of selfish addictions. But this does not change the objective fact of their selfishness, nor does it remove the sense of guilt and doubt that naturally accompanies both intentional and involuntary selfishness. Stating that alcoholism is an illness and not a character flaw is a helpful therapeutic distinction, but it does not relieve the alcoholic of the guilt and doubt experienced as a consequence of destructive behaviors accompanying the disease. That is why Alcoholics Anonymous insists on confession and restitution as necessary steps to recovery.

Most of us evidence commitments of a Stage One and Stage Two variety concerning some aspects of our lives. We may do little more than daydream about status and lustful practices, for example, but we will do anything to make our lives more secure. Such a person might eat and drink moderately, and might be faithful to his spouse, but he will attempt to guarantee his security by spending thousands of dollars a year on health insurance, life insurance, cancer insurance, home insurance, burglar alarms, watch dogs, storm shelters, firearms, etc. It is not that any or even all of these items are unreasonable expenses; the question here has to do with our level of preoccupation with a self-indulgent activity — especially insofar as we are balancing these concerns with our concern for others. Life insurance policies are certainly not diabolical in nature, but every dollar we spend on life insurance and other securities is a dollar that could perhaps have served God in other ways. This kind of consideration is gradually forgotten as our commitment to a selfish behavior becomes a preoccupation and, later, an obsession.

On a final note in this section, we might recognize that what holds true for the individual holds true for families, communities, and even nations. One might ask, for example, whether our pursuit of national security has become a Stage Four obsession, or whether what we call American honor is really not a concern for esteem gone awry. It's something to think about.

A Healing Response

So what can we do about selfishness, especially if it is such an intrinsic and insidious part of our nature? Can anything be done about people who are addicted to some kind of selfish behavior? Also, if there is such a thing as a devil trying to tempt us into selfishness, is not the battle lost even before we begin? These are the kinds of questions we must struggle with if we are to grow spiritually.

We cannot delve into these questions here. But there are numerous other works that deal with such matters, one of them being my own book *Becoming a New Person* which utilizes the Twelve Step program of self-help groups as an aid to overcoming selfishness in our personal lives. What I would like to do here is to examine what a Christian response might be to the five causes of selfishness. This reflection will be brief, but perhaps it will catalyze continuing reflection in the reader.

1. *Self-preservation drives,* especially as they relate to our

physical and psychological needs, are recognized by Christianity to be legitimate. Rather than denigrate this basic part of our humanity, Christ calls us to balance them with a love of neighbor. Our pursuits of pleasure, esteem, and security become destructive when they make us negligent of the needs of others. '' . . . love one another as I have loved you,'' commanded Jesus (John 15:12). That this love must include concern for others is powerfully stated in his parable of the Last Judgment (Matthew 25:31-46). Those who have cared for the needs of others will be saved; those who have been contemptuous of the needs of others will be damned. Thus it is that Christ calls us to identify our well-being with the well-being of other people.

2. *Environmental forces.* Those of us who know of homes where parental abuses are hurting children must make an effort to intervene if we want to consider ourselves Christian. If nothing else, we must try to find a way to help abused children learn to grow — perhaps through schools and churches. Christians also ought to actively oppose all environmental influences that promote consumerism, narcissism, hedonism, and other forms of selfishness. If we cannot do this through political means (such as banning the sale of pornography), then we must do everything possible to help our children understand the subtle temptations in these messages. Media advertising is one area where parents and schools can do more to ''inoculate'' our young people against manipulation. But we ourselves must first recognize the risks and learn how the media are seducing us into buying things we don't really need and embracing values that aren't really Christian.

3. *Physical and mental illnesses.* Jesus healed wherever he went, and he told us that we would receive this same power from him (Mark 16:18). This refers not only to faith healing but also to the efforts through which the scientific and medical community can heal. We need to support research that seeks to understand illnesses; only food, housing, and education ought to receive as

much funding as research. But knowledge is not enough; we need to take sick people to places where they can get help. This may sound obvious, but the fact is that there are over nine million alcoholics in our country who have not had professional help. There are countless others suffering from neuroses and psychoses who have not received help. Many of these people will be intervened on later — by the criminal justice system, perhaps after taking an innocent victim's life. They need help before the problem reaches such a drastic stage.

4. *Stress*. There are no better remedies for stress than prayer and a simple lifestyle, both of which are emphatically promoted by Christianity. If we took quiet time each day to still ourselves before God, we would become less anxious about ourselves and the future. If we sought to possess no more than we truly need, we would not have to stay in jobs we hate in order to make the money necessary to support our affluent lifestyle. '' . . . do not be anxious,'' Jesus states time and again (see Matthew 6:25-34). He himself possessed very little, yet his joy was without bounds.

5. *Sin*. ''Submit yourselves therefore to God. Resist the devil and he will flee from you,'' wrote Saint James (4:7). Although its power is great, the devil cannot make us do anything we do not want to do. The devil tempts us mainly by utilizing natural means such as the media or our stresses. As charitable secular humanists have shown, it is possible to live a good life without a commitment to religious faith. Still, there is no getting around the fact that the power of the Holy Spirit can help us to resist the devil and live unselfishly. That is why Saint James did not say that we must only resist the devil, but that we must submit to God first. Without the power of the Holy Spirit, our best intentions can easily become distorted by the power of sin and degenerate into selfishness.

How do we get plugged in to the spiritual power necessary to overcome sin? Through faith. How do we get faith? That's what Chapter 5 is all about.

Reflection/Discussion

1. What does self-love mean to you? How is it different from selfishness?
2. How does selfishness show up in your own will-to-pleasure, will-to-esteem, and will-to-security?
3. Give some examples of selfishness occurring on a national level.
4. Which of the five causes of selfishness (instinct for self-preservation; the human environment; physical and mental illness; stress; sin) afflict you most often?
5. What do you believe about sin? What do you believe about the devil?
6. What kinds of behaviors in your own life correspond to each of the four stages of selfishness (anticipation; experimental indulgences; habituation; necessary indulgence)?
7. What are some steps you can take to reduce selfishness in your own life? What can you do to reduce it in the world?

2

The Challenge
of Scientific Materialism

We know that the whole creation has been groaning in
travail together until now; and not only the creation, but
we ourselves, who have the first fruits of the Spirit,
groan inwardly as we wait for adoption as sons, the
redemption of our bodies. (Romans 8:22-23)

During my graduate student days, when I was studying and
doing research in evolutionary biology, I attended a seminar with
another grad student whom I shall call Steve. I was drawn to Steve,
for we were the only two among scores of students and professors
who publicly struggled with the religious implications of our
profession. It was not unusual to find Steve commenting, during
seminar discussions, on the spiritual nature of human beings or on
the moral dimensions of population control or genetic engineering. In this sense, Steve was most refreshing; the problem was that
our colleagues did not take him seriously. Steve was a biblical
fundamentalist who believed in scientific creationism.

As time went on, a most distressing development began to
separate Steve and me. At first we enjoyed getting together over
coffee and talking about Jesus, prayer, and moral issues. But,
inevitably, our discussions began to focus on the theory of evolu-

tion. There was no doubt in my mind that Steve loved the Lord and that he was trying to live a life of love. But somehow Steve's understanding of how God works in the universe excluded regard for the theory of evolution. Because Steve had found his way to Christ through a fundamentalist community, he valued their teachings immensely — almost as though their doctrines were responsible for his faith. To reject their teachings regarding scientific creationism would have thus constituted a rejection of his faith — which was the pearl of great price in Steve's life. Although I did not at that time have a sound grasp on these kinds of issues, I knew that the answers were not as simple as Steve was making them out to be. I was also concerned about his credibility among our colleagues and their growing conviction that religious people were out of touch with the "real world."

I tell this story about Steve because I believe it illustrates a split in our culture that is the source of a tremendous erosion of religious faith. It is not a new story, to be sure. Galileo, Newton, Darwin, Marx, and Freud have been dead for decades, but we have not yet thoroughly assimilated the theological implications of their findings. Although the poor and ignorant peoples of the world could hardly care less about the kinds of issues Steve and I were struggling with, the influence of scientific materialism continues to divide people of good will in the educated societies of the world.

Scientific Materialism

Scientific materialism is an attitude that emphasizes completely natural and rational explanations for the origin and development of the cosmos. By defining scientific materialism as more of an attitude than a philosophy, I do not mean to imply that there are no philosophies promoting its message. Our concern in this chapter will not be with those philosophies but with the assumptions that underlie them.

There are two fundamental assumptions about reality common to all forms of scientific materialism. The first assumption is that all phenomena in the universe are ultimately explicable in terms of their material components and the ways these components inter-relate with one another. The interrelationships of these components can be comprehended and interpreted according to the laws of physics and chemistry, which we are now mastering at an unprecedented rate.

The second assumption is that human reason alone, especially when it is disciplined according to the norms of the scientific method of inquiry, is sufficient to discover, analyze, and interpret the laws of the universe.

The approach of scientific materialism is reductionism. Large, complex phenomena are broken down into smaller components, which are in turn broken down and analyzed. The human mind is therefore a consequence of brain functioning, which is a result of nerve impulse transmissions, which in turn build on nerve cells and neurotransmitters, etc. If you doubt the dependence of the human mind on such substructures, observe the deterioration of mental functioning in a person who suffers from Alzheimer's Disease. Deficiencies in acetylcholine, an important neurotransmitter, cause the Alzheimer's victim to become absentminded, dis-oriented, and, eventually, insane. Thus, conclude the reduction-ists, mind is merely the result of the functioning of certain nerves and chemicals.

Because it is believed that complex phenomena can be explained in terms of the simpler ones that preceded them, scientific mate-rialists have followed their reductionistic inquiries backward through time via the theory of evolution and even to the beginnings of the universe, the Big Bang. Although they are quick to admit that evolution and the Big Bang are scientific myths, they none-theless affirm them as superior to religious myths about creation. "The chief difference between them and our modern scientific myth of the Big Bang is that science is self-questioning, and that we can perform experiments and observations to test our ideas,'' wrote Carl Sagan in his book *Cosmos*.

The theory of evolution in particular has been a hard pill for theologians to swallow. Not only did it call into question the six-day account of creation prevailing during Darwin's time, but it also posited a world in which the complexification of life occurred because of chance mutations. Biblical scholars have pointed out the mythological nature of Genesis, making it possible now to accept that evolution took place over millions of years. But the fact that genetic mutations seem to take place according to random and chance factors has been an almost insurmountable problem for theologians to explain. This single factor has kept many scientific materialists away from religious faith because they find it irreconcilable with belief in a Creator God.

Many people who have acknowledged the theological difficulties presented by chance mutations have continued to affirm that our Creator God has worked through evolution to bring creation along. They believe that the structure of matter itself made it possible for evolution to take place and that it was God, after all, who created this matter in the first place. In this kind of response, God's role in creation can be noted directly in the creation of the universe and indirectly through evolution.

At first, the Big Bang theory of the universe seemed to affirm this response. The theory caused Pope Pius XII to exult. Physicists, he said, have proved that God has created the universe. Not everyone, however, sees it that way. Other interpretations of the Big Bang do not necessitate a supernatural origin. For example, what if the superheated, primordial matter-stuff out of which the galaxies and quasars exploded was the result of a compression-crunch of a previous universe? This is entirely possible. Many physicists believe that there is enough matter in the universe to eventually halt its expansion and cause it to gravitate back into itself. What if the universe has been doing precisely that — expanding and contracting — for trillions of years? One still might ask where the first universe came from. But note that direct evidence of a Creator God has been pushed even farther back.

Another "natural" explanation for the Big Bang has it that the primordial stuff dropped out of another universe via a black hole of some kind. Again, one might inquire about the origin of the mother universe, pushing the question of God's creative role another step back. But what if that mother universe is entirely different from ours? What if it has entirely different physical laws so that the whole question of time and beginnings becomes totally irrelevant? We are engaged in idle speculation, of course. But that is precisely how scientific materialists view our own religious convictions concerning God's role in creation. "If we wish courageously to pursue the question, we must, of course ask next where God comes from," wrote Carl Sagan in *Cosmos*. "And if we decide this to be unanswerable, why not save a step and decide that the origin of the universe is an unanswerable question? Or, if we say that God has always existed, why not save a step and conclude that the universe has always existed?" If we did this, scientific materialists could then shake off any need for the supernatural to give rise to the natural. They would be "home free," their basic assumptions about reality left unchallenged.

Scientific materialists demand rational answers to the kinds of questions raised by evolution and the Big Bang. In response, theologians have often taken a defensive position. "But there must be a God! Everything suggests it!" they plead. And when the scientific materialists respond that we are being superstitious and irrational, we often become even more defensive. One such defensive response — scientific creationism — will be discussed shortly. For now, we must simply acknowledge the manner in which scientific materialism erodes religious faith by removing the necessity of God from the universe. In the face of this reductionist attitude, one is left feeling as though belief in the purposefulness of life is only wishful thinking and that religious faith is at best only a personal crutch or irrational superstition.

Scientific Creationism

"The central issue in science and religion today is whether nature in its evolution has any purpose or ultimate meaning," writes John Haught in *The Cosmic Adventure*. "It is questionable whether our own lives can be seriously taken as deeply meaningful unless the cosmic context of these lives is itself imbued with purpose," Haught concludes.

Scientific materialism calls into question the objectivity of purpose. According to this viewpoint, the only purpose our lives have is a purpose we decide to give them; outside our minds there is no objective purpose to life. And as we have seen, the human mind is a mere consequence of nerve impulses from the cells of the brain. It is easy to understand why many people have reacted negatively to these claims. One such reaction has been scientific creationism.

The basic strategy of scientific creationists has been to formulate a theory concerning the origin and development of life on earth that is sympathetic to — if not dependent upon — a literal interpretation of the Genesis account of creation. This is sloppy science, at best, forcing data into a predetermined mythos; still, there is no doubt that most evolutionists do the same.

Scientific creationists propose that the world and its life forms were created almost instantly by a Supreme Being, that a great flood once destroyed a myriad of species that previously existed, and that the age of the earth and human history is nowhere near the millions of years which geologists claim. They point to inadequacies in the theory of evolution such as gaps in fossil records, inadequacies in our geological dating techniques, and the disappearance of large groups of life forms followed by the appearance of new forms. Pointing to these gaps, creationists deny the evolutionary view: the idea that life forms changed gradually through long periods of time and that this fact accounts for the diversity of species we see today.

Scientists are aware of all the issues raised by creationists, and competent biologists have no difficulty responding to the issues they raise. Our concern here is not with the creationists' ''scientific'' assertions but with their effort to salvage purpose in the universe in the face of the scientific materialist assault on faith.

We should be immediately suspicious of any scientific theory that is promoted by any group of people who have a specifically religious bent. The fact that most scientific creationists also happen to be biblical fundamentalists immediately shows what we are dealing with here. We may find scattered nonfundamentalist scientists who have been recruited to affirm one or more of the points raised by creationists, but, by and large, creationists interpret creation through the eyes of biblical fundamentalists.

Even if creationists could successfully defend the world view of Genesis through scientific means, their main contention — that a Supreme Being is the cause of creation — is not a testable scientific hypothesis. Why not two Supreme Beings, one might ask? Since most nature religions are polytheistic, why not attribute creation to twenty gods?

Scientific creationism has not caught on because it is scientifically compelling; it has caught on because it is a valiant attempt to retain purpose in the cosmos. It is a reaction to the scientific materialism of our day which questions how we can speak of purpose in any objective sense. But creationism is an attempt which must fail. In the first place, Christians should not interpret the Genesis account of creation literally. Second, we cannot salvage religious meaning at the expense of scientific truth. My fundamentalist friend, Steve, was unable to gain the respect of our agnostic colleagues because he would not acknowledge certain facts about the universe that are basic to science. These scientists wanted nothing to do with a God who would demand intellectual dishonesty.

If what evolutionists say about the origin and diversification of life on earth is in keeping with the available data, the challenge to Christians is to explain what the first chapter of Genesis means when it says that God is Creator. I do not believe the Church has done a very good job at this. Teilhard de Chardin tried to teach us that God is present within and outside of matter, guiding creation from within and without. In response, the Catholic Church silenced Teilhard and reaffirmed Genesis. This silencing was not helpful to the millions of Christians who are trying to understand how their faith in a Creator can be understood in the light of evolution. The Church's reluctance to address this issue properly is largely responsible for the narrow-mindedness of many scientific materialists today. It might also have provoked fundamentalists' desperate attempt at understanding which is expressed in scientific creationism.

The present challenges remain the ones which Teilhard was trying to address. How do we explain to today's world our belief in a Creator? What are we to make of the many accidental forces which shape the earth's history, such as hurricanes, earthquakes, volcanoes, meteorite collisions, ice ages, etc.? What about genetic mutations? These mutations take place because of a seemingly accidental array of causes. They have very significant implications concerning evolution. These and other questions raised by the theory of evolution have been addressed by theologians, but I do not believe a healthy understanding exists among the faithful. Until there is a better response to scientific materialism than scientific creationism, we can expect the continuing erosion of religious faith among millions, who inevitably find their way to some form of selfishness and/or secular humanism.

A Critique of Reductionism

In beginning our response to scientific materialism, it will be necessary to examine its assumptions about reality and to give credit where credit is due. Fidelity to the truth demands that we do so, and scientific materialists will not respect us if we avoid this task. This is another area where creationism has failed. In place of an adequate response, creationists have launched a defensive attack on the shortcomings of scientific materialism without regard for what truth there is in its methods and conclusions.

To begin, we must admit the obvious truth: reductionism has helped us to better understand the manner in which physical reality is structured and operates. This kind of knowledge has benefited everyone in terms of medical technology, nutrition, communications technology, energy, etc. Reductionism opened the door to a higher standard of living by giving us greater power to manipulate physical reality to our own ends. In so doing, it has also put to rest all kinds of superstitions about the way Nature functions. We might even say that reductionism has "tamed" Nature, displacing its mysteriousness with simple cause-effect explanations. Natural phenomena might not be completely predictable (as those who observe weather forecasting know too well), but they are certainly comprehensible in terms of a few natural laws.

These are very strong points in favor of reductionism, and it is easy to understand why many would look to its approach as the key to understanding all of reality. Indeed, it is difficult to argue with the kinds of results achieved by the reductionist approach because it has been so successful and because its primary opponents — mainly the ignorant and the superstitious — have been proven wrong on so many occasions. Nevertheless, it is possible to argue the limitations of reductionism without even resorting to dogmatic assertions about revelation or pointing to gaps in the data.

One of the most compelling arguments against reductionistic absolutism is advanced by Paul Davies in his popular book *God and the New Physics*. Davies finds no scientific evidence for or against belief in a Creator. But he does point out that the reductionist approach is oblivious to the phenomenon of holism. "Reductionism," states Davies, "seeks to uncover simple elements within complex structures, while holism directs attention to the complexity as a whole." He goes on to emphasize the importance of a holistic as well as a reductionistic approach to understanding.

What Davies means by holism can perhaps best be explained by examples. At the molecular level, we find molecules behaving differently than a mere summation of their atomic parts. Reductionism could never have predicted that hydrogen and oxygen would form so peculiar a molecule as water. Yet, reductionism can identify the hydrogen and oxygen, measure its mass, describe its chemical bond, analyze its characteristics, etc.

On a cellular level, reductionism can tell us what's in a cell and how the organelles are working. Reductionism can also tell us why certain cells become sick and what cells require in order to survive — information which has greatly improved our lives. But reductionism cannot explain why certain peculiar arrangements of the right molecules produce a kind of matter capable of irritability, movement, and reproduction — in short, life. Holism recognizes the fact that cells are not only composed of simpler subunits but also organize matter to suit their needs. Living matter has the unique ability to complexify other matter by acting upon it through behavior, digestion, excretion, etc.

We see this most clearly when observing the functioning of the human mind. It is true that the mind is dependent upon the brain with its nerve circuitry and neurotransmitters. But it is equally true that mental functioning *determines* the kinds of signals running through the brain, determines hormone levels, and even determines whether we breathe and eat. Without a healthy mental attitude, physical health suffers. Reductionism cannot account for this kind of interdependence between mind and matter. Reductionism maintains that mind is a natural consequence of a complex organization of matter. This is true, of course. But it is not the whole truth.

A holistic critique of reductionism helps us to recognize different hierarchical levels of reality, each of which builds on the simpler while exerting influence over it. John Haught, in *The Cosmic Adventure,* follows the lead of many philosophers in referring to a physical level, a chemical level, a living level, and a mental level. He writes: "Our mental processes depend for their successful achievements upon the reliable workings of biotic and physiological functions in our bodies, which in turn rely upon chemical processes. The latter in turn rely upon physical laws which themselves are orderings of quantum occurrences." So far this is reductionism pure and simple. But Haught also states: "The higher levels do not interrupt or interfere with the lower. That is why they cannot appear or be understood at the level of the lower." Thus mind is a phenomenon in its own right, even though it depends upon brain cells and neurotransmitters for its functioning.

If it is true that the phenomenon of life cannot be observed and understood at the level of atoms with their different kinds of quarks, then why should we expect to be able to locate the fullness of God within the limitations of our human mental abilities? If God exists in a hierarchical level that transcends our own, then the reductionists' contention that God's existence cannot be proven is a mere truism. One does not find a higher level of reality fully manifest in a lower level. This is why physics, chemistry, and biology are separate sciences, although they are surely interrelated. Paradoxically, these are the disciplines in which scientific materialism thrives. Yet, no biologist hopes to comprehend the mystery of life by studying the behavior of subatomic quarks! Why, then, should any scientist fall prey to the arrogance of reductionistic absolutism? Why maintain that God cannot exist simply because there is no evidence in support of this belief? To take that stance is to proceed as though God were just another piece of data that we could wrap our minds around as we do, say, a white rat. God, if he exists in a higher level of reality, can no more be comprehended by a human mind than a circle can comprehend a sphere or a sponge comprehend the *Summa Theologica* of Thomas Aquinas. The only way such a God can be known is through his self-revelation in minds that are open to receiving it. Such mental opening is what faith is about.

The Limitations of Reason

The function of reason in science is to establish cause-effect relationships between pieces of data. These data must be accessible to the senses; they must be measurable in some fashion if they are to be useful at all. Thus it is the function of reason in scientific materialism to interpret causal relationships between sensate data. The process for establishing these causal relationships is the scientific method of inquiry.

Again we must acknowledge the awesome powers of reason unleashed in this approach. Human reason, disciplined by the scientific method of experimental verification, has helped to unravel some of the mysteries of physical reality. But, as with reductionism, the absolutizing of this mode of reasoning turns scientific materialism into a pitfall to spiritual growth.

The first objection against this idolizing of human reason is that it relies completely on physical data that is accessible to the senses. The assumption here is that what is not sensate does not exist; or if it does exist, it is purely subjective and probably illogical. Since God cannot be isolated as a piece of sensate data, then belief in God is irrational. Our discussion of hierarchical levels above disclosed something of the absurdity of this kind of thinking. Sensate reality does not fully account for psychological phenomena such as thoughts — much less for the existence of God.

Any scientist who is honest will admit that the best ideas come about not as a consequence of logical deduction but of creative intuition. Did the data alone suggest the theory of evolution to Darwin? Of course not! Taken as a whole, Darwin's findings suggest chaos. It was Darwin's mind that inferred the logical implications present in his data. It was Darwin's *intuition* — that most unsensate of mental equipment — that found a creative way to organize the data. Intuition is responsible for the hypotheses and theories which the scientific method seeks to verify or discredit. Why, then, should any scientist seek to minimize the role of intuition when it suggests the possibility of a higher dimension of reality impacting our familiar world?

Then there is the question of feelings and their supposed subjectivity. Scientific materialism places such a high premium on rationality that it minimizes the role of feelings in life and even in science. Abraham Maslow once pointed out that the reason Konrad Lorenz was able to note such meticulous details about the behavior of geese had to do with Lorenz's love of geese. This love made him more interested in them — hence, more observant and more objective. And one must surely love the night sky to sit before the telescope for hours gathering ''objective'' data about what goes on out there.

Since it is obvious that intuition and feeling play such vital roles in the service of objectivity, one must ask why scientific materialists become so critical when feeling and intuition suggest the existence of dimensions of reality that are not accessible to the senses alone. I believe John Haught is right on target when he speaks of the ''modern anti-hierarchical ideology'' as the epistemology of control.

It is essentially our obsession with power that leads us to think that whatever is real must somehow be subject in principle to mastery by our own intellects. The epistemology of control is simply the carry-over of the will to power into the realm of the mind. It is a refusal to acknowledge the possibility that there are fields of reality that lie off limits, even in principle, to the control of rational consciousness. To open ourselves to such a possibility would require a renunciation of our impulse to control. And this is too high a price for many of us to pay.

Haught and many others suggest that the historical origins of this kind of pride (we are back to narcissism) can be traced to the fierce struggles for intellectual liberation fought by scientists against equally proud dogmatic theologians a few centuries ago. After the scandal of Galileo in particular, scientists — many of whom had begun their careers in seminaries and religious colleges — became distrustful of all religion with its myths and superstitious legends and rituals.

Happily, those days are gone, and we can see quite clearly the important role that science has played in helping to rid religion of its magic and superstitions. Because of science, we have today a purer form of religion than at any time in history. Faith can no longer be based on those God-of-the-gaps apologetics so popular even a couple of decades ago. Science has filled in many of the gaps (or else promises to do so soon). Nevertheless, we are still a long way from witnessing the kind of cooperation needed between science and religion if civilization is to survive. Having extricated itself from vulnerability to the ethical critiques of religions, science has accumulated knowledge in an ethical vacuum. In this day and age when nuclear technology threatens to eliminate a supportive environment, and genetic engineering offers near-godlike powers, scientists and religious need to work together in humility and openness.

Chance Factors

Holism and a critique of the limitations of sensate reason show how belief in God can be squared with scientific materialism. But the problem of chance occurrences and the role they play in the evolution of the universe remains untouched. For example, we know that atoms radiate particles or waves in a random fashion. This radiation might strike a DNA molecule and alter the structure of a gene on the molecule. This genetic alteration will work for better or (the usual case) for worse. If the altered gene enhances survival and is passed on through reproduction, it will become part of the population's gene pool. These kinds of mutations appear to be very common, and their occurrences are due to chance factors. This is why scientific materialists question the whole notion of a providential Creator.

Several objections against the role of chance in evolution have been raised, most of which are easily thwarted by competent evolutionists. One such argument, based on statistics, maintains that the odds against chance mutations eventually producing a human brain are infinitesimally small. But as Carl Sagan has pointed out in response, the odds of a meteorite falling through someone's roof are also small. And the odds that this would happen twice to the same person are practically nil. Yet that is precisely what happened to a woman in Australia. On two different occasions a small meteorite fell through her roof. Statisticians who would maintain that this could not have happened because of the overwhelming odds against it would have to "eat crow." It happened — and it demonstrates that one reality offsets a billion probabilities to the contrary. Similarly, chance mutations and chromosomal aberrations *do* account for changes in the structure of DNA and, consequently, in organisms and populations. We *do* have brains — so, chance mutations must have played a vital role in the evolutionary line leading from protozoans to human beings.

Another argument has it that chance could no more have produced a brain than a monkey could sit at a piano and, by chance, play Rachmaninoff's Second Piano Concerto. But this objection, too, is based on a misunderstanding of the evolutionary process. The human brain was not thrown together in an instant out of a chaotic collection of matter — as we are requiring of our musical monkey before the keyboard. The human brain developed from a less complex primate brain, which evolved from simpler ones, etc. Tissues did not develop until cells were in abundant supply. Cells could not exist until chemical evolution had proceeded to the extent of forming an abundance of the large complex molecules that became part of the cell's microstructure. Macromolecules did not develop until the earth's crust and atmosphere had attained sufficient stability so as to prevent their dissolution. Complex dimensions of reality built upon simpler levels only after the simpler ones had become diversified and stable. No doubt there were millions of molecular arrangements that did not produce cells, but a failure did not necessitate starting the universe all over again with the Big Bang. "In evolution distinct levels have emerged, each one of them eventually falling into stable, repetitive and predictable routines," notes John Haught in *The Cosmic Adventure*. "And like notches of a ratchet, the existence of these stable levels (the sub-atomic, atomic, molecular, biotic, psychological) prevents the wheel of Nature from going back to point zero with each turn."

Using the analogy of our musical monkey, evolution could produce Rachmaninoff's Second Piano Concerto by "saving" each correct note, even though that note was struck by chance. The monkey would not be required to begin anew after each mistaken hit but could proceed, note by note, until this complex and masterful work was completed. In this view, there is a strong probability that given enough time our monkey could indeed luck out each note. In such a manner could chance mutations, time, and the conservative nature of matter and living tissue eventually produce a human brain.

But where is the creative hand of God to be noted in this vision? Some would maintain that God is directly responsible for the mutations and other ''chance'' phenomena that help to bring about novel arrangements of matter and living tissue. Our next chapter will examine this option more fully. For now we will lay it aside, noting only that more often than not chance mutations result in unfavorable changes. To maintain that God is responsible only for the helpful ''chance'' mutations and not the harmful ones is to get a bit silly. Surely, there must be a better way to include God in the creative process.

Unfortunately, there are no scientific or even philosophical observations which absolutely necessitate the existence of God to explain evolution. There is, however, a position that recognizes the role of chance while admitting the possibility of an extraneous dimension of reality guiding evolution along. Once again it is John Haught and his reflections on the process philosophy of Alfred North Whitehead who has helped so much to bring clarity to this issue.

Using the analogy of a stream flowing through a countryside, Haught points out that the width, turbulence, and speed of water flowing in the stream are not determined so much by the chemical nature of water as they are by the landscape through which the stream flows. He says: ''Though non-energetic itself, the form of the landscape is a determinative factor in the amount of energy available in the river's flow. . . . The landscape's energetic passivity is not easily made the subject of explicit knowledge as long as we are focally concerned with the flow of water. And yet the energetic potential and activity of the stream is itself a gift of the landscape.''

In this view, scientific materialists would be like people who examine only the water without acknowledging the influence of the landscape on its behavior.

But what if God is like the landscape in the above analogy? If we look at evolution this way, the stream of evolution could still proceed as described by scientific materialists. Chance mutations and other factors would derive from the inherent properties of matter itself. But they would be molded by the extraneous and "passive" influence of God. God would be the One who provides the necessary molding influence. Out of the multitude of ways in which matter is arranged, God would conserve the line of complexity that leads to life and mind. And if we further concede to God the creation of matter that is capable of stability and novelty, then the traditional vision of God as Creator would be complete.

Our understanding of the universe does not preclude such a direct role for God in the creation of matter. And our understanding of evolution becomes more intelligible by bringing in the notion of a God who landscapes the mold through which matter can develop. As a result, there is no need to fear that scientific materialism can debunk religious faith. Nor should we try to debunk the sound conclusions of scientific materialism by resorting to probabilities, statistics, forced analogies or — especially — scientific creationism.

As a means for understanding what is taking place in the stream of evolution, the reductionist approach of scientific materialism is unsurpassed in its clarity and honesty. But in order to comprehend something of the landscape through which this stream flows, we need the insights of those people of faith who have, through the ages, greatly enriched our lives with meaning.

The God Within

A multidimensional approach to reality allows us to do two things. First, it lets us accept the findings of scientific materialists.

Second, it allows us to admit that materialist conclusions are limited only to those dimensions of reality that are open to scientific investigation. God's life transcends the kind of data scientists can gather — which is why God cannot be observed directly through scientific investigation. Science can examine only God's *effects*. Belief in a Creator God is not ruled out by the fact of chance mutations. As a potter molding his clay, God has shaped matter along lines that lead to the complex life forms we see about us today.

Divine influence in evolution need not be merely that of an "outsider God," however. At best, we would be begging the question to claim that evolution has developed along its present lines because God laid the forms through which unstable matter could complexify. This view would be an improvement over the deist idea that a disinterested God created matter and then simply allowed it to run its course. But we would still have a view in which God works on evolution strictly from the outside. That God would not really be *involved* with matter, would not be incarnational. Such a God might counter the scientific materialists' denials of God's place in evolution. But that God would not meet the criteria of intimacy demanded by Christianity.

But how could God be more involved in evolution than by molding its form from a position of transcendence? The answer to this question must be that God works from the within of matter as well as from without. God's creative Word not only shapes matter from without but "inspires" its development from within. At this point, scientific materialists would probably accuse us of bringing up the old arguments of vitalism. But we do not need to resort to vitalism to explain the divine influence. God's influence within matter itself makes a great deal of sense if we accept a multi-dimensional view of reality.

According to scientific materialists, the magnificent diversity of life forms we find about us today resulted from chance mutations that somehow helped certain animal groups become better adapted to their environments. For example, certain fish developed primitive limbs and crawled onto land where food was plentiful and competition minimal. The development of feathers from reptilian scales made it possible for birds to glide (then later fly) away from predators. Behavior, in this viewpoint, develops according to the anatomical possibilities present in an organism. Matter determines behavior. This belief accounts for the discomfort felt by most scientific materialists with any notion of freedom in human beings, much less lower animals.

But what if we reverse the roles of behavior and anatomy, and assign to behavior a primary role in evolutionary diversification? What if, for example, natural selection favored the development of limbs in certain fish groups because these fish "wanted" to crawl out of the water? What if birds developed feathers and wings because they "wanted" to fly? What if, long ago, a certain primate group began to develop a large brain because its members "wanted" to learn? In each of these cases, the behavioral impetus would provide the organizing principle around which selection could act on chance mutations to improve the anatomical structures for carrying out the behavior in question.

At this point scientific materialists will surely accuse us of being teleological — of thinking that organisms have built-in ends or goals toward which they tend. But that is no reason to suppose that we are being unscientific. Many behaviors are determined by genetic factors, so it is possible that the behavioral initiatives mentioned above might also derive from genetic factors. Assigning to behavior a primary role in evolution does not, therefore, lead to an escape from materialism altogether. It does, however, surface a new dynamic in the diversification of life.

Now suppose we back up one step further. Let's go back to a point *before* the selection of genes that give an organism its behavioral impetus. What if God provided the creative spark that preceded even the selection of a certain gene for behavior? In this view, God could have inspired the evolution of the cosmos from within matter and life as well as from without. Using our analogy of the musical monkey, we might say that God put it in the "heart" of the monkey to play music — and that, after making this selection, God "saved" the genes for behavior and anatomy that allowed the monkey to play music. An "interior" view such as this would allow us to affirm the Judeo-Christian conviction that the creative Word of God is at work in creation.

As with all things pertaining to God, it is impossible to prove that God's immanent inspiration and transcendent molding influence caused evolution to proceed along the lines it has taken. But neither is it possible to disprove such a position! People of faith demonstrate to us the irrefutable fact that the inspiration of God helps to influence human thinking. Therefore, human behavior, which is governed largely by thinking patterns, is, in many people, shaped by divine inspiration. It may well be that this kind of interplay between divine inspiration and human behavior is at this very moment in history continuing to shape the genetics of human behavior. There is no reason for us to believe that we have finished evolving.

Could lower life forms or inanimate matter receive inspiration from God? A hierarchical view of reality suggests that this is possible. Each level in the hierarchy possesses some rudimentary degree of internal freedom. Most significantly, I believe, the mystics of all religions have stated that the Spirit of God pervades all of reality.

Summary: An Emergent Universe

The cosmos described by scientific materialists has been called a resultant universe — a result of millions of years of chance arrangements of matter. Among those arrangements, one peculiar

59

line — the one that gave rise to life — complexified through the years. In that resultant view, the possibilities inherent in the universe are entirely determined by the nature of matter. Therefore, in that view, the only way to understand this universe is to understand the matter which causes its stability and complexity.

In a resultant universe, life forms have a present and a past but no definite future. They have arrived at this point in time because of the organization of chance factors and because of successful competition with other life forms in an ever-changing environment. The future of living organisms will depend on how new chance mutations and environmental factors interact. When we contemplate the future of planet Earth, free human behavior figures in only to the extent that we influence the stability of living matter by disrupting the environment. As with the past, any future complexification of living matter will be strictly a consequence of accidental factors. A resultant universe is therefore a closed universe. It cannot grow into anything unless it creates something new from within itself.

The resultant universe view of scientific materialism is a source of great hopelessness today. Hope requires a future into which we can cast our hearts. But the world view of scientific materialism presents us with nothing but a blind alley. As Teilhard de Chardin once wrote, ''Worldly faith, in short, is not enough in itself to move the earth forward. . . . '' But, Teilhard went on to ask, ''can we be sure that the Christian faith in its ancient interpretation is still sufficient of itself to carry the earth upward?''

Teilhard's response — like that of Whitehead and others such as Charles Hartshorne and John Haught — offers us the concept of an emergent universe. Haught writes: ''An emergent universe is an evolutionary one in which each successive phase adds something qualitatively new.'' Haught further maintains that ''The emergent phase is more than the sum of its antecedents. . . . In an emergent universe the influence of extraneous formative causation is the ingredient required to channel the mass-energy continuum into novel and ontologically distinct levels of being."

Many scientific materialists are perfectly willing to acknowledge the influence of a higher dimension of reality upon a lower. But they are not willing to admit to the possibility of a "highest" level of reality that embraces even the human mind. In an emergent universe this highest level — God — is the creative molding force within and outside of creation.

In an emergent universe time takes on new meaning. The past reveals the ingenuity in which chaotic chance occurrences are woven into patterns of ever more novel complexity and order. Because of this process we can rest assured that God will continue in the future to salvage every bit of creation that can be gathered into his creative fold. Nothing will be lost (John 6:39). In fact, we can look forward to even more novel assimilations than we now observe. We can have a basic sense of trust in reality and a hope that creation will eventually unfold according to the vision of beauty inspired by God.

This vision of an emergent universe seems to be in keeping with the view of the New Testament writers. It also contradicts nothing in the findings of scientific materialists. Christ is seen as the "image of the invisible God, the first-born of all creation; for in him all things were created, in heaven and on earth, visible and invisible. . . . " (Colossians 1:15-16) He is the Alpha and the Omega, the first and the last (Revelation 21:6).

From the dimension of reality in which he resides in risen splendor, Christ now touches all of space and time. Since his Resurrection, all of history — even those millenia which preceded him — has been thoroughly permeated with his saving presence. He is the next rung in the ladder of our evolutionary history; he makes it possible for us, as psychophysical beings, to become spiritualized selves (see 1 Corinthians 15:39-53). Our destiny is filled with the promise of glory.

Reflection/Discussion

1. Scientific materialism has two underlying assumptions: *one*, that all phenomena can be explained in terms of their material components; *two*, that human reason by itself can know the laws of the universe. Has either of these assumptions raised any doubts of faith for you? If so, what form did these doubts take?

2. This chapter claims that scientific creationism is not science and is not good theology. What is your response?

3. Evolution seems to be filled with events that happen by chance. Please explain how you reconcile this apparent fact with the concept of a Creator.

4. Do you believe God already knows the future? What role does God play in influencing the shape of the future?

5. What part of this chapter has challenged you most? Why?

3

The Challenge
of Suffering and Evil

So we do not lose heart. Though our outer nature is
wasting away, our inner nature is being renewed every
day. (2 Corinthians 4:16)

Incident 1: A friend of mine, Mike, recently learned that his
father has lung cancer. The cancer is already quite advanced, and
there is little hope that Mike's father can be saved. "Dad quit
smoking five years ago," Mike lamented. "You'd think God
would have honored his decision!" Mike went on, blaming God
for what was happening.

Incident 2: My wife, Lisa, asked her sixth-grade religion class
whether they understood why so many people are starving in
Ethiopia these days. Several of the children in the class stated that
the Ethiopians are starving because they are probably not Christians. Other children in the class assured Lisa that God was
punishing the Ethiopians for something they had done wrong.
Many of the children said that this is what their parents had told
them.

Incident 3: Driving home the other night, I was listening to a
radio preacher explain the meaning of Thanksgiving. According to

the preacher, it was God who had sent the storm which blew the pilgrims bound for Jamestown off course, forcing them to land at Plymouth Rock. God, the preacher said, had previously eliminated the Indians in the area by sending a plague, so the pilgrims did not have to worry about Indians. The winter cold brought the pilgrims extreme hardships and many deaths. But these tragedies, too, were part of God's plan, the preacher maintained.

Incident 4: John and I are only professional acquaintances, but the other day he decided to share with me some of his religious doubts. While we were lunching with friends, John brought up the tragedy in which a madman shot and killed twenty-one people at a McDonald's restaurant. "I just don't see how God could have allowed that," John objected. "Either God can prevent evil but won't, or he wants to prevent it but can't." Before I could respond, another acquaintance jumped in, saying, "Maybe it was their turn to go; God works in mysterious ways, you know!" John shook his head in defiance. There was no discussing the issue any further.

I share these stories because they are typical of the ways in which many people try to make sense of suffering and evil. All these examples share the common assumption that God is directly involved in human affairs in such a way that he causes the circumstances — both good and bad — that happen to us throughout life. Several writers even go so far as to say that bad and good are really only relative terms — that what we consider evil might, in the long run, really turn out to be good. Thus "God works in mysterious ways." To this way of thinking, God's concern is with the big picture of our developing universe, not with our petty hopes and the circumstances that frustrate them.

Most people have never heard the word *theodicy*. Webster defines it as the "defense of God's goodness and omnipotence in view of the existence of evil." That is what the incidents mentioned above are concerned with, and that is what this chapter is about. Our approach here will be to examine the assumptions about God that underpin the thinking described in the four above incidents.

In the area of theodicy the tradition of the Church is remarkably rich; writers and thinkers through the ages have developed a body of Christian wisdom that has helped many people to deal with such questions. Despite that rich tradition of theodicy, however, I find massive confusion among most people when it comes to this issue. One of the saddest consequences of this confusion is that it keeps many people from turning to God when they need him most. Sad as it is, the situation is understandable. After all, why seek anything from the One who is the ultimate cause of all our troubles?

Causes of Suffering

No one needs a definition of suffering. It is, quite simply, the pains we bear as we go through life. We all know a lot about suffering, but it may be helpful to distinguish between the different sources of our pain. In another book, *Jesus Alive in Our Lives* (Ave Maria Press, 1985), I discuss four common causes of suffering: self-inflicted pain, social shortfalls, growth, and accident/chance. Let us briefly examine the differences between these causes.

1. *Self-inflicted pains* derive from our own mistakes. Poor eating habits, smoking, and lack of exercise are examples on the physical level. Heart attacks and cancer can result from these poor habits. Guilt and shame which result from lying and other immoral behaviors are also self-inflicted. The point here is that *we do it to ourselves*. Happily, we can reduce self-inflicted pains with discipline and a little help from our friends.

2. *Social shortfall pains* happen to individuals who live in an imperfect society — which means all of us, to one degree or

another. Viewing society as a social organism, we might say that these kinds of pains are socially self-inflicted. They are caused by other people, or else are not prevented by those who have the means to do so. War, crime, and even famine are cases in point; they are the results of human behaviors, and so they can be reduced or even prevented altogether.

3. *Accidental pains* refer to those myriads of seemingly chance occurrences which hurt people and which cannot be prevented. A wave of radiation can start a cell on a cancerous route or cause a birth defect, a lightning bolt, a blowout in a tire, an earthquake, or a tornado — all examples of occurrences about which we have not the slightest foreknowledge. There is much we can learn about these phenomena, but their activities usually lie outside the influence of human willpower.

4. *Growing pains* derive from our natural tendency to stretch our physical and psycho-spiritual boundaries as we get older. They are part of life. From the birthing process, to learning to walk and talk, through adolescence, aging, and death, pain accompanies growth. These pains cannot be prevented unless one decides not to grow. But even then, a failure to grow causes pains of its own.

These four causes of pain often come together, forming intense and complicated patterns of suffering. During our lives we all suffer from all four of these causes — usually from a combination of them. There is *dukkha* — suffering — in the world. This is the first of the Buddha's four Noble Truths, a teaching that finds echoes in the Christian belief in Original Sin. Life is dislocated, like an axle that is off-center from its wheel or like a bone that has slipped out of its socket. But, as we shall see, sorting out the sources of our pains can help us to cope better and even to grow in faith during our most painful times.

The Nature of Evil

We have examined four common sources of human suffering. But what are its origin and "objectives"?

Let me begin on this question by saying that I believe evil exists. I believe, for example, that Adolf Hitler was an evil man, not merely a misguided politician. I also believe that there are many evil people in this world, and that most of us are evil at least at some time during our lives. As M. Scott Peck put it in his book *People of the Lie*, evil exists when an individual or institution uses its power to oppress others for the sake of preserving its own sick identity structure. This oppression is real, and it is destructive.

The major religions and great philosophers have struggled for centuries with the problem of evil. According to one view, evil springs from an Evil Spirit that is equal in power to the Good Spirit of the universe. This view is called *dualistic* because it claims there are two root causes of reality. It finds classic expression in the ancient Persian religion of Zoroaster and in its offspring, Manicheism, which strongly influenced the thinking of Saint Augustine in his younger days.

On the other hand, in several religions there are pantheistic interpretations which view all of reality as God. Some interpreters in this vein have theorized that there is really no such thing as evil — that what we regard as evil stems merely from our limited point of view. Accordingly, something that we regard as evil might, in the long run, be necessary to bring about greater good. God, in this view, is mainly interested in bringing about a maximum of good in the universe; if a few people need to be crushed in the process, then so be it — the end justifies the means.

Secular humanists, meanwhile, consider evil to be the consequence of ignorance. "No man willingly chose falsehood over truth, or evil over good," wrote Abraham Maslow, echoing Socrates.

Christianity does not embrace any of these notions of evil.

In his classic novel *The Brothers Karamazov,* Dostoevski tells his famous parable of The Grand Inquisitor. In this parable the question is raised whether God could condone the progress of good in the universe if it required the slaughter of an innocent child. To this question Christianity answers an emphatic NO!

Christianity is a religion of means. Means determine ends, and crooked means cannot produce straight ends.

In their masterful *Dictionary of Theology,* Karl Rahner and Herbert Vorgrimler speak of evil as ''not only an absence of the good but an express and decisive renunciation of the good. . . . the organized attempt of the individual, of peoples, of the world as a whole, at self-sufficiency within this world.''

Evil is a consequence of rebellion against goodness. But goodness, according to Christianity, is the more powerful principle because Jesus has risen from the dead. Thus evil is not inevitable, as it is in dualistic and pantheistic thinking. Still less is it the consequence of ignorance alone, as in secular humanism. Evil has to do with rebellion against goodness — usually for the sake of preserving some kind of identity structure which goodness would have us change. Evil is a consequence of selfishness — usually narcissism.

Although evil is partly definable, it is more difficult to unravel the circumstances that unleash the power of evil in the world. I believe Scott Peck has made a great contribution toward this end in *People of the Lie.* Malachi Martin's book *Hostage to the Devil* is also revealing. What both authors point out is the insidious capacity for evil in people and institutions when they meet the following conditions:

1. Avoidance of self-criticism; unwillingness to admit to mistakes. *Perfectionism.*

2. The rationalizing of defects, often by appealing to virtuous "extenuating circumstances." *Lying*.
3. The *scapegoating* of defects onto others through the psychological mechanism of projection.
4. Concern for a public image of respectability. *Pretense*.
   To these I would add one more:
5. Emphasis upon one side only of a contrasting pair of values — for example, justice over mercy, thinking over feeling, organization over spontaneity, etc. *Lack of balance*.

When any of these conditions exist, oppression is not far off. When all of these conditions exist in an individual, other people (especially children) who are close to the person will suffer immensely because of the powers of evil unleashed in their lives. When these conditions exist in an institution — especially in a government — countless people will experience some kind of oppression.

We all know individuals who manifest one or more of these criteria in their lives; certainly it is not difficult to find them festering in most governments. Tragically, the suffering visited upon humanity because of evil is one of the oldest of human stories.

People possessed by evil spirits manifest all the characteristics of evil described above, but to an extreme degree. Evil is the law of their lives. But an evil spirit cannot move in and possess a person unless that person accepts its presence, unless that person has already deliberately laid the mental groundwork to allow evil spirits an incarnational foothold. God has not given evil spirits permission to overpower our own human will. Even if they had such permission, it is doubtful that they could do so anyway. So it is scapegoating on our part to blame human evil on the devil. As the story of the Fall of Adam and Eve demonstrates, the evil serpent only tempts; it does not overpower.

Evil, then, is a consequence of the misuse of human freedom. The sufferings it brings are of the *self-inflicted* and *social shortfall* types. Evil has nothing to do with growing pains or with accidents, because those two sources of pain do not derive from a misuse of human will.

Approaching the matter from another angle, Xavier Thevenot, in his book *Sin: A Christian View for Today,* points out that theologians distinguish between *physically endured evil* (for example, the physical handicap of blindness) and *moral evil* (sin). As the major religions agree, it is in our nature as creatures to undergo failure and suffering, to see our "best laid plan" go awry. These types of suffering are consequences of our human condition.

On the other hand, pain does arise partly from reacting badly to physical evils. Sufferings such as blindness, for example, can become occasions for bitterness toward God instead of being occasions for deepened faith and humility.

At the social level, evil arises when people exploit and manipulate one another. This is the stuff from which sin creates its "body" in the world — stabilized patterns of evil which influence people's lives. Gustave Martelet puts it well when he says: "It is evil becoming an organic presence within individuals and within the world. It is the spiritual misery of humanity, in the form of structures we have fashioned or acquired, taking control of us even though it is a product of our own freedom." The *Handbook for Today's Catholic* describes the same reality when it says: "Patterns of evil can be institutionalized. Injustice, for example, can become part of a group's way of life, embedded in laws and social customs. Such patterns, in a ripple effect, contaminate the attitudes and actions of people in that environment. The influence of these patterns can be so subtle that people in them may literally be unaware of the evil they promote."

"This organized tearing-down of the fabric of life exacts its toll in human suffering," observes Xavier Thevenot. "And on top of that, another problem arises from the fact that some people mistakenly blame this body of sin in the world on 'life' or 'Mother Nature,' when what it is in reality is sin embodied in the world. It is, for example, a mistake to call Black Lung — a condition that has destroyed the health and lives of generations of American coal miners in Appalachia — a mere 'occupational hazard.' '' There is an ongoing tendency to confuse the two levels of evil: the *physical* evil we experience as a result of our human limitations — and *moral* evil, a result of our human freedom.

It is interesting to note that Christian symbolism also recognizes the evil wrought by Satan to be a consequence of the misuse of freedom. The influence of Satan and other evil spirits is among us precisely in order that we, too, will use our freedom to deny God's goodness and assert our own self-sufficiency.

Can God Prevent Evil?

All of this leads to the questions asked by Mike and John in Incidents 1 and 4 at the beginning of this chapter. Rephrasing their questions now, we might ask: Why does God permit evil to happen? Why doesn't God prevent self-inflicted suffering and social injustice?

These are tough questions. Let us reword them in order to get to the core of the issue: What would God have to do in order to prevent evil from happening?

The evil we are discussing is the natural and logical consequence of the misuse of freedom. So, the only way to prevent self-inflicted and socially destructive behaviors would be to limit our freedom to choosing only the good. But this would be no freedom at all! We would be mindless automatons, with no independent will.

In his best-selling book *When Bad Things Happen to Good People,* Harold Kushner provides this helpful analogy:

Imagine a parent saying to a child, "How would you like to spend this afternoon, doing homework or playing with a friend? You choose." The child says, "I'd like to play with my friend." The parent responds, "I'm sorry, that's the wrong choice. I can't let you do that. I won't let you out of the house until your homework gets done. Choose again." This time the child says, "All right, I'll do my homework."

This "solution" would eliminate the sufferings we experience because of evil, but it would not leave us free. Indeed, it would make of God an evil authority; God would be exerting power over us against our will. Or, to put it another way, we would be extensions of God with no real life of our own.

The answer to the question of God's role in evil is that God has nothing to do with evil. God is love; and we, who are created in God's image and likeness, are free to accept or reject his love. Love cannot exist outside of a context of freedom. God does not want our love to be a blind, instinctual drive but a decision made in freedom. This is a unique privilege; no other animal (much less plant) is free to embrace its Creator so consciously. But neither are other life forms free to reject God as we are.

God created us free to accept or reject his love. He knew that most of us would reject him some of the time, and that a few would be contemptuous of his love most of the time. He must have known that the gift of free will would enable men like Hitler to rise to power (thanks to the thousands who allowed this to happen). He also knew that the Cains of this world would kill the Abels and that madmen would be able to gun down innocent people in fast-food restaurants. Yet, God nurtured the evolutionary process along to the point when humans could, finally, in spirit and truth, choose to love him in return. Why does God allow evil? He must have decided that the few who would accept his gifts and grow to the fullness of human stature would make it all worthwhile.

Just because God allows evil does not mean that God approves of it, however. *God loathes human evil!* Christ's position was always to resist evil without further escalating it. Through his death and rising, Jesus broke the decisive hold of evil in this world, demonstrating that the power of goodness is stronger than that of evil. We see, then, that God's goodness is not nullified by the fact of evil in our world. We see, too, that God's power is not negated by evil, for the risen Jesus established a spiritual beachhead from which all of creation shall eventually be renewed. Although evil remains a harsh reality in our world, it could be eliminated in a short time if all people freely turned to God for the grace to live in truth and love. Because we do not do so, evil remains with us.

Can God Prevent Accidents?

We can make some sense of the fact that God permits moral evil. But there is still the question of God's role in accidental suffering. One might say, "OK, so God had nothing to do with Hitler's rise to power nor with the gunning down of people at McDonald's. But why didn't he at least warn those who would be in McDonald's at that fateful instant? Why doesn't he warn us about earthquakes or tornadoes or tires ready to blow out? He would merely be giving us information; this wouldn't preempt our freedom nor the integrity of our love for him. So why, if he is so good, does God not prevent accidental pains by forewarning us?"

One common response to questions like these is to say that accidental occurrences are part of God's plan. The twenty-one people who were shot in McDonald's were *supposed* to be there at that instant. Those who got there later because they had been held up by a traffic light or because their lunch period was later were *not* supposed to be there. In this way of looking at it, there is no such thing as chance or luck. As the radio preacher put it, the storm that blew the pilgrims to Plymouth Rock was really the "breath of God."

I do not believe this view of accidental suffering is consistent with belief in a good God, as my friend John rightly noted. For example, if God sent the storm that blew the pilgrims off course, then God must be held equally responsible for the deaths that followed from the winter hardships. There is also something especially repugnant in the thought that God sent a plague among the Indians to prepare the way for the pilgrim settlers. Christianity does not permit such a view of God, not even in the interests of his power and providence.

But what are we to say, then? If God is not directly responsible for accidental pain, then who is? And aren't we really saying that God has no power to prevent accidents?

Before responding to these questions, it may be helpful to note that accidental pains — tragic as they may be — are not necessarily evil. Although destructive (to us), a storm has no willpower to use in contempt of God. Storms, plagues, viruses, and earthquakes operate in nature according to laws which can be comprehended and, in some cases, even anticipated. The only way in which God might be implicated in such matters would be if God directly caused these natural occurrences. Then would God be like the madman who sprays bullets into a crowd; his weapons, in this case, would be lightning bolts, storm clouds, volcanoes, and vermin. Christian theology does not take this view of God's workings in nature.

Many of the circumstances we call accidental are not really accidental at all. They are all perfectly explainable in terms of nature's laws. Let us consider a few examples.

1. *Earthquakes* can often be predicted. Geologists are capable of identifying unstable areas as high risks. In the very near future,

geologists may even be able to issue earthquake warnings before a quake. People who live in unstable areas should not, then, speak of an earthquake as an accidental occurrence. If half of California were to fall into the sea tonight, it would be an immense tragedy, but no geologist would be surprised.

2. It is a well-known fact that *lightning* rods help to protect a building. Individuals can also escape damage from lightning by going into a car or a building. It may not even be appropriate to speak of the path taken by lightning as accidental. If we had sufficient data concerning the electrical charges in clouds, trees, buildings, etc., we could probably predict the exact place where lightning would strike.

3. *Radioactivity* which causes cells to become abnormal is often considered accidental, but there is little doubt that people who spend lots of time in the sun are more likely to get skin cancer. Radiation from food, water, and the air we take in is also somewhat controllable, though not entirely. After all is said and done, radiation may be the most pure form of accidental circumstance, since all elements radiate particles and waves in a seemingly random pattern as they undergo natural deterioration.

4. *Blowouts* in tires can probably be eliminated completely by constructing better tires and improving quality-control testing. Today's tires, while not perfect, are considerably more reliable than those sold even a decade ago.

5. *Viruses and bacteria* have just as much "right" to be here as we do. When we take them into our bodies through food or water, they will grow if conditions are right. Although we cannot eliminate these factors, we can reduce their destruction through hygienic practices, good nutrition, and vaccinations.

Much of what now causes accidental suffering may one day be eliminated because of improvements in technology or greater care and efficiency. If the pilgrims had set sail for Jamestown in 1985, they would have had access to better weather forecasting and cartography and so could have adjusted their course accordingly.

Can God prevent accidents? We must say that there is a sense in which God can prevent them, but that there is another sense in which he does not do so. God does not prevent accidents by suspending nature's laws, but God has given us a mind capable of understanding nature and bettering our condition in the environment. God allows us to experience the natural consequences of our place in nature; to do otherwise would be to deny us that place. If God warned us every time a tire was ready to blow out, we would never have had the initiative to build a better tire or to improve our highways. We would probably never do anything about the social problems involved if God forewarned us of the approach of a madman with a gun. Starving peoples present us with an opportunity to better distribute the world's nutritional resources and technologies. If God stepped in and suspended nature's laws or forewarned us when problems arise, we would learn nothing and do nothing about them. We would cease to grow individually and socially.

Our experiences of accidental pain are not without explanation, but this does not change their tragic nature. People who suffer from such accidents are no more deserving than those who escape them. The Christian response to tragedy is simply to be with those who suffer and then to work to prevent tragedy from happening again.

What About Growing Pains?

Even if we could eliminate all forms of self-inflicted, social, and accidental suffering, we would still have pain. There is a suffering that comes with our movement from birth to death, and no member of the human family can escape these growing pains. They are a bond we all share in common, an integral part of our basic humanity.

Growing pains come as we stretch our physical and psycho-spiritual boundaries. For the infant, birth itself is painful; so is being hungry, constipated, sleepy, and bored. Cutting teeth is painful. Learning to crawl, walk, talk, and use the bathroom is difficult, too. The first three years of life involve tremendous growth on the physical and psychological levels, and so it is there that we find the most pain. Any parent with small children can attest to this; learning to nurture young ones through their painful times is one of the most difficult of all parenting tasks.

Parents of adolescents often state that they believe puberty to be an even more painful time than early childhood. The adolescent experiences pain self-consciously, and is usually (especially in the case of boys) trying to fulfill a stereotype that views pain as undignified. Trying to pretend that they "have it all together," many adolescents repress their confusion and insecurity. It's a crazy and bewildering time of life, but, thank God, it finally passes.

My grandmother is ninety-one years old. Her bodily organs are beginning to fail, one by one, and it is likely that she will die very soon. She has not felt healthy and strong for years. The death of my grandfather two years ago did not make things easier for Grandma. Yet she suffers bravely and without complaint. She is grateful for the gift of life that is still hers, but prepared to die when the time comes. The other day she told my mother, "It's not dying that's hard; it's getting there." Growing pains shall follow us to the grave.

Some people curse God because of these kinds of pains. They bemoan the fact that we experience any kind of pain at all. "Why not a different kind of experience to accompany growth?" they might query. In his novel *Catch Twenty-Two,* Joseph Heller has one of his characters ask why not a bell instead, or a flashing light of some kind, to take the place of pain?

Pain is a mystery. No one really understands why some people hurt more than others or how the brain interprets pain. It is obvious that pain is intended to stimulate us to change certain behaviors which are presumably not good for us. Would the infant ever rub its gums to help its teeth break through if the gums were not irritated? Would the adolescent ever grow into a healthy identity if he or she never experienced confusion? These questions tell us something of the survival value of pain, but they do not answer Joseph Heller's question: Why pain at all?

All we can say is that growing pains come with life and that's the way things are. We may not like it, but that's really beside the point. *Growing pains come with life.* Those who believe in God experience them just as atheists do. One may therefore choose to believe in God and suffer or to doubt God's goodness and to suffer. I do not see the advantage of disbelief when growing pains are viewed thus.

Could God have created a world in which no one would experience growing pains? We do not know the answer to this, of course. But there is something in this very question that often spills over into ingratitude for the great gift that life really is. Certainly life is difficult when one suffers, but most of us do not experience such excruciating pains very often. Life, for all its pains, is usually quite tolerable. Given the right attitude, life can even be enjoyable. That's where faith comes in.

The most significant religious question concerning growing pains and other kinds of suffering is not "How could God allow such a thing?" but "How shall I suffer?" If we complain and rebel against our pain, burdening others and fighting against reality, things only get worse. Suffering turns us inward and tempts us to selfishness, which only deepens suffering.

Redemptive suffering requires that we persist in our commitment to love God and neighbor even when we are in pain. It means suffering without complaint, just as Christ suffered from social injustice and growing pains without complaint. Redemptive suffering can deepen one's compassion for others and bond us together as a human family. American and Russian children both hurt when they cut their teeth; everyone is afraid to die. Yet, if we suffer together bravely, we often find, like Christ, new life on the other side of our pain.

Christianity and Miracles

Theodicy is concerned with explaining how God's goodness and power can be understood against the backdrop of the suffering and evil in our world. Thus far we have seen how we can understand God's goodness in such a way that it is not invalidated by human evil, accidents, or natural growing pains. We have noted that God's use of power to shelter us from these kinds of pain would amount to a major suspension of the laws of nature or else a preempting of human freedom. God leaves us free to accept or reject grace, and allows us to experience the consequences of our own natural and cultural vulnerabilities. Like a parent who allows her child to take a few lumps and bruises from life on the path to maturity, God leaves us vulnerable in our freedom.

But we have not yet taken into account certain phenomena considered to be miraculous. By miracles I mean phenomena that go against the usual operation of the laws of nature. Many instances of faith healing cannot be explained by doctors. Christ's calming of the storm (Matthew 8:23-27), walking on the water (Matthew 14:22-33), and his multiplication of loaves and fish (Matthew 14:13-21) are also cases in point. The ''problem'' with such miracles is that they seem to indicate that God can (and does) sometimes intervene in such a manner as to transcend nature's laws. For many theologians, such miracles confound the tidy conclusions reached above because they admit that God can intervene in human affairs if he wants to, which means that God does indeed spare certain privileged people the painful consequences resulting from accidental and even evil circumstances. The questions which then arise are: Why doesn't God, if he is so good and powerful, intervene through miracles more often? Don't miracles indicate that God is somewhat capricious in demonstrating his goodness and power?

One common response to these questions is to deny that miraculous occurrences take place at all. For example, Louis Evely, in his book *The Gospels Without Myth,* attempts to explain miraculous phenomena described in the Bible in terms of completely natural occurrences. The miracle of the loaves and fish was not really a multiplication of food but a magnificent potluck picnic. According to Evely and others, Jesus' example of love and gratitude inspired the people to break out the morsels of food they had kept stashed away in their clothing. When everyone made their stashes available for distribution, there was plenty to go around.

Others have chosen to interpret the miracles of Jesus as merely symbolic statements by the evangelists. The multiplication of loaves and fish is viewed as a prefiguring of the Eucharist. The healing of blind people is regarded as a statement of how Jesus can heal our own spiritual blindness. The raising of Lazarus and others is a symbolic reference to the Resurrection of Jesus and the new life he brings to those who believe in him. Even the Resurrection of Jesus has not escaped such ''demythologizing.'' Many have welcomed such conclusions because they simplify the task of theodicy.

Rather than attempt a comprehensive response to the issue of demythologizing the miracle accounts in the Bible, suffice it to say that such conclusions are anything but final. Debate over this issue is sure to continue for years to come. Our concern at this point is theodicy and the special problems raised if we concede the point that miracles have and still do take place.

I believe in miracles. I also believe there are different kinds of miracles. Faith healings, for example, are often considered miracles — and I believe they are. I have been present when sick people were cured through the laying on of hands. I have observed chronic alcoholics recover from their fatal illness because of the spiritual renewal they experience through working the Twelve Steps of Alcoholics Anonymous.

But there is a sense in which many faith healings are really "natural" occurrences. The faith of the recipients puts them in touch with the mentally stabilizing influence of a higher dimension of reality. Just as a healthy cell is able to organize molecules to serve its needs, a spiritualized mind is better able to govern a body. (This insight may account for the conclusion in many cultures that sickness is caused by an evil spirit.) In some people there are pockets or areas of stress and neurosis that prevent mental energy from tending to the needs of the body. When a person's mind is attuned to spiritual reality through faith, the block between mind and body does not exist; energy can pass from mind to body. This is surely part of what happens in faith healing.

But, just as surely, there is much that remains mystery. The unconscious cancer patient who is physically healed when bathed in the waters of Lourdes does not fit the above "natural" explanation of faith healing. The alcoholic who is healed through practicing the Twelve Steps fits it more closely.

What the above "natural" model of faith healing is intended to indicate is that God need not be considered capricious when it comes to faith healing. It is God's will that all people come to know him through faith. It is also God's will that we all benefit from the mental and physical energies increased in us through faith. Many people have noted that converts actually appear younger after coming to God in faith! Worry wrinkles often fade away; psychosomatic problems become minimized. But faith does not remove us from the natural consequences of aging, nor ought we to expect that faith will shield us from accidents. The "natural" benefits that come to us because of faith do not eliminate the natural consequences imposed upon us by life in the body on planet Earth.

A very dear friend of mine, a woman of deep and abiding faith, is currently dying of cancer. Recently she told me that she expects God to heal her because she is certain that it is God's will that no one suffer from cancer as she is suffering. "God does not want anyone to die of cancer," she concluded. I asked her how she thought God wanted us to die — if there was a painless way to go out. "God wants us to die of old age," she responded, "or else of a heart attack while sleeping," she added, chuckling. My response was that there is no such thing as death by old age; there is only death when organ systems fail, and this can happen at any age. As my ninety-one-year-old grandmother has taught me, organ system failure late in life is a very painful experience — possibly as painful as dying of cancer in middle age. Dying of a heart attack might spare an individual suffering, but the loved ones left behind will have to suffer because of the severed relationship and all the unfinished business that remains.

There is no easy way to die. Even though faith can help our minds and bodies perform at their optimal levels, we still must die. Faith does not make it possible to stave off organ system failure forever. Even people who are cured through a faith healing of some kind go on to die later in life — often from a malady as painful as the one from which they were cured. What faith makes possible is redemptive suffering — the ability to continue to love even while in great pain. After all is said and done, this is the greatest miracle of all.

The nature miracles of Jesus are qualitatively different from faith healings, however. Storm clouds, bread, fish, and water are incapable of opening themselves to a higher dimension of reality. Such miracles would require the *imposition* of a higher level upon a lower in a manner that goes against the usual course of Nature. That is why it is held that these kinds of miracles attest to a capricious kind of influence by God upon Nature.

But why should we be disturbed if God has indeed intervened in Nature by calming a storm or multiplying loaves and fish or raising Jesus from the dead? Why would such interventions cast a shadow of doubt over God's goodness? Suppose, for example, I gave my young daughter the task of baking bread for our family. Suppose I provided her with everything she needed for the task, and then allowed her (and me) to suffer the consequences for better or worse. At first she would find this task difficult, but she would improve as time went along. Then suppose one day I decided to go out and buy a loaf of bread to surprise her and to show her that I support her in her responsibility. Would such a gesture on my part indicate that I am capricious?

Similarly, I find God's goodness in no way enriched by negating the nature miracles of Jesus. Just because he once multiplied loaves and fish, it does not follow that Jesus is callous because he does not work another miracle for people starving today. What is normal is that we should strive to feed ourselves by using the talents that God has given us. What is normal is that we should experience hunger when food resources are scarce. We should expect no more than this kind of bargain from life. Any departure from this course of events would therefore constitute a rare and special occurrence. The multiplication of loaves and fish should likewise be interpreted as a rare and special manifestation of God's generosity among us. This kind of gift is undeserved, and should inspire us to gratitude that it was ever given at all rather than ingratitude that it does not take place more often. We should be thankful that we once experienced an "acceptable year of the Lord" (Luke 4:19). We should be encouraged that, through the miracles and Resurrection of Jesus, God has shown that he supports us and is with us as we strive to carry out our tasks in building a better world. We would be immensely more hopeless and despairing if we had never received from God such special manifestations of his goodness.

Although Jesus revealed a God who possesses power greater than Nature and even death, we should never forget that this same God is well acquainted with the sufferings we experience during life. In Jesus we meet a God who has suffered the full range of human pains but who has not sinned (Hebrews 4:14-15). The fact of suffering and evil need not lead us to doubt the existence of God, still less God's goodness and power. Were it not for the revelation of Jesus, we would be overwhelmed by the immensity of suffering and evil in our world. Because of Jesus, however, we have reason to believe that "the sufferings of this present time are not worth comparing with the glory that is to be revealed to us" (Romans 8:18). Because of Jesus we have reason to hope for new life even as this present life falls into decay (2 Corinthians 4:16).

Reflection/Discussion

1. What source of pain do you suffer from most: self-inflicted, social, accidental, or growing?
2. How do you view God during your times of suffering?
3. Do you hold God responsible for the sufferings and evil in this world? Why? Why not?
4. What does God do to help us diminish suffering and evil?
5. How do you feel about miracles? Do you believe they take place? If so, what do they tell us about God?

4

The Challenge
of Secular Humanism

> But understand this, that in the last days there will come
> times of stress. For men will be lovers of self, lovers of
> money, proud, arrogant . . . holding the form of re-
> ligion but denying the power of it. Avoid such people.
> (2 Timothy 3:1,2,5)

Q. What kind of person does one become if science is viewed as
the way to all truth, if there is no such thing as sin — only
ignorance — and if, consequently, certain kinds of selfish
behavior are condoned?

A. A secular humanist.

The above question and answer will make sense to you especially if you have read Chapters 1 through 3 of this book. Everything we have discussed thus far has led to this point.

It is my opinion that secular humanism is the most insidious and
dangerous source of doubt in today's world. Why? Primarily
because it builds on the three sources of doubt we have just
discussed.

It is insidious because it so thoroughly pervades our culture and
seems, on the surface, to be an admirable approach to life. And it is

dangerous because it can lead us to believe that sustained goodness is possible without reference to God.

But what, precisely, do we mean by secular humanism? To hear some fundamentalists talk, one would conclude that a secular humanist is a liberal Democrat. Being somewhat of a moderate Democrat myself, I am certain there is much more to it than that! Many liberal Democrats have arrived at their political convictions through a discernment process illuminated by faith. This is not true of secular humanists, even though their political convictions are often identical to the convictions held by people of faith.

For the secular humanist, faith does not enter into the process of discernment at all. What is of primary importance is the betterment of the human condition in this world.

But what is wrong with such a noble aspiration?

At first glance, there is nothing wrong with the desire to build a better, more humane world. The only people who do not share this dream are the thoroughly evil. The real issue has to do with how we realize this dream. Christians hold that the Kingdom of God can be realized on earth only by submitting the human spirit to the Spirit of God. Only then will we be able to carry out the ethical agenda implicit in the revelation of Jesus Christ. Secular humanists, in contrast, do not believe a religious approach to life is essential to building a better world. Most secular humanists are ambivalent toward the question of religion. Many are actually antagonistic.

Secular humanist beliefs are difficult to summarize, for there is really no identified group or movement labeling itself as secular humanism. Critics sometimes point to the *Humanist Manifesto* penned by John Dewey as a philosophical rallying point for secular humanists. The American Humanist Association, the American Society of Humanistic Psychologists, and *The New Republic* journal also express secular humanist ideas as a matter of course. What these and other groups propose can be generalized as follows:

1. Human beings are part of nature only. We are merely a product of evolution.
2. The meaning of life is the meaning we give to life. There are no objective standards of behavior which all people are bound in conscience to uphold.
3. Ethical values are culturally relative; they grow out of human experience. As cultures change through time, we must adapt and change our values accordingly.
4. We must rely on ourselves alone for survival and happiness. No God will save us or enrich our lives.
5. The individual person alone is the measure of all things. Laws and institutions exist for people, and not vice versa.
6. All knowledge is tentative. There are no certainties, especially concerning moral issues. Science is the way to the fullness of knowledge, and one must keep an open mind concerning all things.

As any informed Christian will recognize, there is a certain amount of truth in several of these positions. One may also find in them an admirable emphasis on becoming responsible and active in building a society that safeguards the rights of the individual. That is why secular humanism is such an insidious danger! And that is why secular humanists often interpret a religious critique as being anti-individual, socially irresponsible, and anti-intellectual. Some even go so far as to accuse religious persons of promoting an autocratic society populated by mindless dependents.

Historical Perspectives

Humanism has been with us a long time, but the secular manifestation that exists today is a relatively new phenomenon. James Hitchcock, in his book *What Is Secular Humanism?*, provides a comprehensive historical overview of humanism from ancient Greece to the present day. According to Hitchcock, all forms of humanism include the study of the place of human beings in this world. They engage in this study with a view to bettering the human lot. Greek thinkers such as Socrates, Plato, and Protagoras developed their humanistic philosophies in a somewhat secular sense. But these philosophers still recognized creation as having arisen from the creative act of a God, however disinterested this deity may have been. They also believed that certain laws governing human behavior could be deduced from a careful study of Nature. This special regard for the Natural Law is most lucidly expressed in the writings of Aristotle, whose philosophy the Church later appropriated through the genius of Saint Thomas Aquinas (1225-1274).

Hebrew and Christian thinkers also developed humanistic philosophies, but in a specifically religious context. Jesus spoke of loving one another and of building a Kingdom on earth as in heaven, but he constantly insisted that one must love God with one's whole heart, soul, mind, and strength in order to realize this vision (Matthew 22:34-40). The early Church seemed to enjoy an intense experience of religious humanism, balancing the love of God and neighbor in a mutually reinforcing dynamic. Love of God deepened a sense of love of neighbor, and love of neighbor intensified love for God. This balance shifted more toward a vertical spirituality through the Dark Ages and Middle Ages, however.

The Dark Ages and the Middle Ages were as otherworldly (indeed, anti-worldly!) a time in European history as one will ever find. Monasticism was promoted as the ultimate spiritual lifestyle; lay involvement in the world was considered a tremendous spiritual vexation. Individualistic spirituality also prospered during this time. Earthly life was regarded primarily as a means of saving one's soul for eternity. Unfortunately, this strong emphasis on individual salvation discouraged one from bettering society or becoming involved in social justice issues. Thus the autocratic cultures of medieval Europe remained the norm until the Renaissance and the Protestant Reformation began to move toward a more horizontal spirituality.

Renaissance humanism blossomed with the rediscovery of Greek philosophy. But most Renaissance thinkers were also believers; their faith prevented them from assuming a thoroughly secular tone. The anti-authoritarianism of Protestant leaders opened the door to a humanism that was free to critique oppressive social structures. Catholic thinkers like Erasmus (1466-1536) and Saint Thomas More (1478-1535) attempted to incorporate the best of Renaissance and Protestant humanism into the authoritarian framework of Catholicism, but it was Protestantism which finally led the way into the democratic, industrialized world developing in the late eighteenth century.

The Founding Fathers of the American colonies carried the humanist agenda forward. Most of them were ambivalent about democracy — they were not sure it could work among a people who were as yet largely ignorant. A compromise between democracy and authoritarian leadership was worked out: the United States were to be a constitutional republic. Even so, this republic was to be a nation under God. Few of the Founding Fathers were deeply religious men; most of them were deists. Still, they acknowledged that humanism and religion made fine partners — provided that no one denomination be endorsed as the official state religion, of course. Among the citizenry at this time, the American spirit of freedom was nourished by deep religious convictions.

Secular humanism such as we find today began in the late nineteenth and early twentieth centuries. It grew out of rationalistic philosophies and scientific movements that swept through the West during this time. The scientific findings of Copernicus (1473-1543) and Galileo (1564-1642) had already dethroned the earth from its position of centrality in the universe, and Sir Isaac

Newton (1642-1727), a man who was as devoted to studying the Bible as he was to science, was being interpreted as upholding the deists' universe. Now came Charles Darwin (1809-1882), challenging the old Creation beliefs by proposing that life forms developed from completely natural factors. Along, too, came Karl Marx (1818-1883), holding that religion is the opiate of the masses, a tool used by the rich to keep the poor in abeyance. Next came Freud (1856-1939), reducing religion to a phenomenon of the unconscious — at best, a neurosis of some kind. This combination of forces from the fields of astronomy, physics, biology, sociology, economics, politics, and psychology gave birth to secular humanism.

Since the late nineteenth century, two kinds of humanism have prevailed: religious and secular. Religious humanism, informed by the Judeo-Christian tradition and unleashed in Renaissance times, continues to inspire hope in millions. But secular humanism has been gaining in numbers and influence, especially since the mid-1960s. Its proponents include a noble list of writers: Schiller, Dewey, Sartre, Camus, Fromm, Maslow, Glasser, Ellis, and many others. Since the mid-1960s, their disciples have unleashed a torrent of self-help books and social critiques promoting the secular humanist way to individual and social happiness. They are responsible for many of the changes that have shaken the Western World, the United States in particular, since 1965.

In the mid-1960s, authority in both Church and State seemed to lose its hold on Americans. The Viet Nam War brought a loss of governmental credibility. So did the ripening of civil rights issues. Vatican Council II (1962-1965) disturbed the smug, unconscious faith of millions of Catholics. Meanwhile, children from the baby-boom era were now becoming adults. Having grown up accustomed to getting what they wanted, they found narcissism and hedonism infinitely preferable to commitment and self-sacrifice. The glue of authority that held American society together seemed to dissolve. Religious humanism lost much of its hold. Secular humanism, once largely ignored by the masses, began to find a receptive audience — thanks to exposure and, in many cases, promotion through the mass media.

This brief historical sketch surely suffers from gross simplifications and generalizations. Still, I believe it helps us to recognize the relative newness of secular humanism. The sketch also points out the debt secular humanism owes to scientific materialism, which we discussed in Chapter 2.

Impact on Christianity

Secular humanist influences have brought about drastic changes in the Church since the 1960s. Darwin, Marx, and Freud challenged the premises upon which religious humanism was based; Christian theologians have been on the defensive ever since. Secular humanist positions were eagerly embraced by many theologians, who attempted to reaffirm traditional dogmas concerning sin, grace, and salvation in the light of secular humanist principles. The results, as we shall see, have sometimes been disastrous.

Although the influence of secular humanism within the Church cannot be discussed here comprehensively, we can easily identify three important changes in Christian beliefs and practices which are due largely to secular humanist writers: the birth of the Social Gospel; a shifting away from Natural Law morality toward situation ethics; and the death of the forensic metaphor of salvation. These three changes all derive from the attempt to incorporate secular humanist teachings into Christianity. Let us briefly examine each of these shifts. Later, we will reflect upon some of their pitfalls and contributions.

The birth of the Social Gospel marked the beginning of the demise of the old privatized Christian spirituality which prevailed in the Middle Ages and persisted in Catholic circles into the 1960s. This shifting away from a strictly vertical spirituality was a healthy sign, to be sure. From the late nineteenth century, popes and councils of Catholic bishops began to speak out on social conditions such as the rights of workers, the plight of the poor, the horrors of war, and, recently, the evils of the nuclear arms race. Protestants had long been involved in these areas of concern, but even they began shifting away from the vertical spirituality that still remained strong in their traditions toward a more social view of the Gospel.

In its extreme form, the Social Gospel emphasizes the primary role of the Church to be one of "humanizing" the world. Jesus came to establish the reign of God among people, we are told; and we, Jesus' followers, ought to be totally involved in helping this Kingdom be realized on earth as it is in heaven. The social dimension of the Gospel is emphasized more than the spiritual. The purpose of Christian teaching ought to be to mold the social conscience, and the primary way to leaven social conscience is through the exercise of Christian prophecy. This is especially called for in situations where certain governments and institutions support policies that lead to the systematic oppression of people. These positions have been expressed most clearly by the writers of what has come to be called Liberation Theology. Some, at least among the lesser representatives of Liberation Theology, seem to agree with that part of the *Humanist Manifesto* which states that ". . . traditional dogmatic or authoritarian religions that place revelation, God, ritual, or creed above human need or experience do a disservice to the human species." To paraphrase theologian Hans Küng, they would say that God's will is the well-being of human beings. Anything that promotes human well-being ought therefore to be endorsed; anything that detracts from human well-being ought to be opposed. It is easy to understand how those who wholeheartedly embrace this viewpoint find themselves sympathizing with Marxist revolutionaries who promise a better world to people being oppressed by a totalitarian regime.

The second broad shift evident in the Church because of secular humanist influences is characterized by the growing disenchantment with moral absolutes based on the Natural Law and a compensating shift toward situation ethics. Natural Law morality was based primarily on Saint Thomas Aquinas' christianizing of Aristotelian philosophy. But life after Darwin, Marx, and Freud brought doubts that God's purposes and intentions could be so clearly observed in Nature as the old moralists had maintained. What if sex, for example, was not primarily a procreative activity but a reinforcement of the couple-bond among human beings? This is what biologists were maintaining on the basis of their study of primates, and this is in part why certain theologians objected so strongly to the Natural Law reasoning concerning birth control found in Pope Paul VI's 1968 encyclical letter *Humanae Vitae*. Situation ethics seemed to offer an inspiring alternative to the old ways of thinking.

The name associated with situation ethics is Joseph Fletcher, who was a longtime professor of Social Ethics at the Episcopal Theological Seminary in Cambridge, Massachusetts. According to Fletcher, what makes an action good is *love*. As he states in his books *Situation Ethics* (1966) and *Moral Responsibility* (1967), "Only one thing is intrinsically good, namely, love: nothing else." In a 1966 article entitled "Why 'New'?" Fletcher gave the following examples: "Lying could be more Christian than telling the truth, since the only 'virtue' in telling the truth is telling it in love. Stealing could be better than respecting private property if, as in eminent domain, the private ownership denies the greatest love of the greatest number. No action is good or right of itself. . . . The new morality, in short, subordinates principles to circumstances, the general to the particular, and forces the 'natural' and the 'scriptural' to give way to the personal and the actual.''

What is good in one circumstance might be bad in another. The struggle to love in the concrete circumstances of life is the noblest of all human activities. In situation ethics there are no moral absolutes from which we can draw prescriptions about what is loving and what is not. As a result, situation ethics with its heavy emphasis on intentions (and not on behaviors) turns morality into a completely subjective matter.

A third shift brought about by scientific materialism and secular humanism has been in the way we present the Gospel. From the early Church on through the mid-1960s, the Gospel was preached as part of what has sometimes been called a forensic metaphor of salvation. Humankind was regarded as sinful and alienated from a good and perfect God. But Jesus, through his death and Resurrection, atoned for our sins and thus bridged the gap between God and humankind. We, for our part, were invited to repent of our sinfulness and, through faith, accept the salvation offered by Christ. It is a simple message, speaking to our sense of guilt before God while holding forth the way to regeneration.

But what if people feel no guilt before God? What do you say to people who regard the doctrine of Original Sin as a myth invalidated by the theory of Evolution? How do you reach the many who, thanks to Freud and the situation ethicists, have come to consider moral guilt an unhealthy feeling — maybe even a neurosis? What do you do when a people have ceased to fear God, and when the fear of God is looked upon as an undesirable sentiment to be banished from the Church? This is the situation facing the Western Church today. Nourished by the teachings of scientific materialists and secular humanists, millions of people today experience no sense of sin in their lives. The forensic metaphor of salvation holds no attraction or promise of hope for them.

I believe part of the success of the evangelical fundamentalists has been due to their ability to reach the many for whom the forensic metaphor of salvation *still* strikes a chord of meaning. The fundamentalists' approach is emphatically forensic, and there are obviously millions of people who are still drawn to God by the simple message of salvation they preach. This may also explain the fundamentalists' distrust of "liberal theologians," who by and large have abandoned the forensic approach to evangelization. In their efforts to make the Gospel "relevant" to today's educated masses, most mainline Protestant ministers and many Catholic priests and catechists have discarded the forensic metaphor and adopted in its place what we shall call the clinical approach to salvation.

The clinical metaphor stresses the "positive" side of the Gospel while downplaying the "negative." It does this in order to avoid "turning people off." Jesus is regarded as the fullness of humanity; he is the definitive model of what it means to be fully human. Clinical preachers love to quote this line from the second-century Church Father, Saint Irenaeus: "The glory of God is a human being who is fully alive." In the clinical metaphor, becoming fully alive is what Christianity is really all about. Love, as they say in Marriage Encounter, is "life-giving." Whatever gives life is therefore loving, and vice versa. (Using these criteria as their rationale, several teachers whom I have heard argue that homosexuality might be a life-giving option for some people. The Natural Law moralists, working from entirely different criteria, could never condone homosexuality.) God's love and mercy are stressed to such an extent that many proponents of this view believe there is really no hell for sinners. Sin is not rebellion but weakness and ignorance. Repentance is minimized; changing "erroneous zones" or irrational modes of thinking is stressed instead. The works of Abraham Maslow, Carl Rogers, Albert Ellis, and William Glasser are enlisted to assist in this attitudinal restructuring. The struggle to love is informed by situation ethics. The practical work of Christianity consists of building a better world. The immensely popular books, lectures, and videotapes of

Norman Vincent Peale and Father John Powell provide as clear a statement of the clinical metaphor of salvation as one will find anywhere.

The emergence of the Social Gospel, situation ethics, and a clinical approach to salvation has brought about significant changes in popular Christian beliefs and practices. Taken as a whole, they characterize Christian humanism as we find it today. Many of these changes, I believe, have been for the better. But many have resulted in destructive consequences the likes of which could not have been foreseen by those Christian reformers who encouraged them. Let us now examine some of the consequences — both positive and negative — that derive from secular humanist influences.

The Fruits of Secular Humanism

An old saying goes, "The proof is in the pudding." Jesus also said, "You will know them by their fruits." (Matthew 7:16) It is only fair to ask: What have been the fruits of the secular humanist emphasis on individual rights unburdened by the moral norms we have inherited from Church, Scripture, and the Natural Law?

First of all, let us look at several positive aspects:

1. The evolutionary perspective taken by secular humanists has given rise to a growing *historical consciousness*. In the past, philosophers and theologians tended to view the world as a static, finished product. Moral norms were based upon essences and principles that were deduced from a close scrutiny of Nature. In contrast to that static, essentialist view, the evolutionary perspective indicates that the world is still in a process of becoming and that human beings have a crucial role to play in that process.

2. *Global consciousness* is another outgrowth of secular human-ism. The environmental movement in particular has helped to make us more aware of the interdependence of all life. If we are to survive on this planet, nations will have to learn to live together; it may even be time to do away with national struc-tures and operate out of a global political structure.
3. The *environmental movement* has helped to raise awareness that we cannot go on polluting our planet and ravaging our resources. The Judeo-Christian tradition had often been inter-preted as sanctioning a form of dominion over creation that hurts the environment. The environmental movement has been influential in leading to a reinterpretation of human dominion as stewardship, an entirely different concept.
4. Strong voices for *civil rights* have been raised by secular humanists. Racism, sexism, ageism, and other forms of preju-dice have been deplored by secular humanist writers, although religious people have also been on the front lines in these struggles.
5. Finally, one must give credit to secular humanist writers for helping millions to grow in self-acceptance and self-love. Many *self-help books* penned in recent years have proven to be a healing aid to people suffering from low self-confidence and mild neuroses. It was, I believe, the success and popularity of self-help writers that encouraged a reframing of the Gospel in the clinical metaphor discussed above.

These are very strong points in favor of secular humanism. All Christians ought to rejoice in the good being done by secular humanists in these areas; all Christians ought to support these causes. It may even be appropriate to say that the work being done by secular humanists in behalf of social justice and personal growth issues is ''God's will.'' Perhaps they are like the people in the Gospel who refused to listen to the Master, then went out and did his will anyway (see Matthew 21:23-27). There is no question that many secular humanists have been more involved in social issues than orthodox Christians. This is, in fact, one of their ongoing criticisms of Christianity.

Unfortunately, however, there is a shadow side to secular humanism that cancels out much of the good it brings about. This shadow side derives from its inability to place constraints on human rights because of its confusion concerning moral norms:

1. A *narcissistic self-sufficiency* often seems to be endorsed by self-help writers. Without a religious context in which to situate one's life direction, self-sufficiency naturally arises as the primary focus of values. Autonomy replaces theonomy as the goal of personal growth. This attitude became pervasive during the 1970s, often called the "me decade."

2. *Sexual irresponsibility* is condoned in the name of sexual liberation. Sex outside of a context of commitment has become increasingly common since the mid-1960s; commitment was regarded as an old-fashioned and even chauvinistic practice. "In the area of sexuality, we believe that intolerant attitudes, often cultivated by orthodox religions and puritanical cultures, unduly repress sexual conduct," states the *Humanist Manifesto*. "The right to birth control, abortion, and divorce should be recognized," it concludes. In the absence of prohibitive social conventions, marriage partners began to feel free to shop around. Unmarrieds, generally, began to experiment with sex before marriage. It is difficult today to find a marriage between two virgins. In fact, many young people are embarrassed to admit that they are virgins.

3. *Abortion* is condoned by virtually all secular humanists, for the right to abortion is held to be an indispensable human right.

Pro-abortionists, therefore, like to speak of themselves as being "pro-choice" — the *mother's* choice, that is. The rights of the fetus are either ignored, or else are downplayed by considering the fetus to be nonhuman. More than any other issue, this one has led to the loss of spiritual health in the West.

4. *Illegal drug use* is acceptable by many secular humanists, who view legal restrictions in this area as another governmental infringement on human rights. Many secular humanists strongly advocate the legalization of marijuana, cocaine, and other drugs, even though it is now apparent that these chemicals do great harm to individuals who take them, as well as to the rest of us who have to live in this world with chemically dependent people.

5. *The right to publish and film pornography* is defended by secular humanists in the name of freedom of the press. "If an individual does not want to look at it, then he or she is free not to," state the secular humanists. "Don't impose your moral standards on us by prohibiting this right," they object.

The kinds of issues listed above are all defended as individual rights. But secular humanists who insist upon these rights seem reluctant to face the reality of the damage done to individuals, families, and, consequently, to society as a whole. The wisdom of the ages has maintained that sex, for example, is such an explosive force that the culture ought to discourage permissive attitudes while encouraging commitment between sexual partners. But in their frenzy to protect individual rights, secular humanists are often callous when discussing the consequences of permissiveness in a culture. Their naïveté concerning sin and the devil further prevents them from concluding that it is often in the best interests of a people to prohibit free and easy access to alcohol, drugs, sex, pornography, and other incendiary forces.

Modern Christian Humanism

In Chapter 3 we noted that one of the factors that allows evil a foothold among us is the overstressing of one side of a values continuum to the neglect of the other. This is, I believe, the problem with secular humanism. Its social agenda emphasizes social justice and the love of neighbor, but deemphasizes love of God. Its personal growth values are pro-individual, but to the neglect of communal welfare. It is difficult to critique either of these issues, however. If, for example, one accuses secular humanists of being callous toward the welfare of the community by supporting such extreme individual rights as the right to abortion, they will quickly point out all the work being done to further social justice. When accused of being socialists, or of supporting social policies that hurt individuals, they point to their work in behalf of individual rights. Yet secular humanist social and personal growth platforms are not so mutually complementary as they might seem. When viewed from a Christian perspective, many glaring contradictions become evident.

Christians and agnostics who have adopted the platforms of secular humanism often experience overwhelming measures of doubt. As we noted in the previous section, secular humanism opens the door to behaviors that are explicitly selfish in origin and consequence. Sexual irresponsibility, recreational drug use, and a narcissistic attitude in one's relationships all lead away from God. Narcissism can become an especially insidious force when it is carried over into the realm of spirituality. The narcissist might seek grace, but only for the "high" it will give. Spirituality is viewed as a natural high and not as a means to know God and discover his will. Conversely, the narcissist seeks God to sanction and energize her or his *own* will.

Another way in which secular humanism has spawned doubt among well-meaning people is through the discouragement that results from its social policies. Many secular humanists believe that poverty, unemployment, famine, and other injustices can be legislated away. Their basic solution to social problems is governmental intervention. They have no understanding of the connection between sin and social injustice. So when government programs do not accomplish what they set out to do, secular humanists become dismayed. The truth is that most government programs make only a very superficial impact on social problems. The underlying sinful realities continue to fester, unresolved and unreconciled.

If Christian humanism is to overcome doubt and become a more potent force for good, we will need to balance some of the excesses deriving from secular humanist influences. In the area of social justice, we will have to become less faithful to Karl Marx and more faithful to Jesus Christ. Our social action guidelines will have to be more rooted in prayer and reflection on the Gospel and less dependent on the *Communist Manifesto*. The social encyclicals of the Church provide a good starting point, but far too few Christian reformers have read these radical documents.

In the social encyclicals we find the right balance between love of God and love of neighbor. Where secular humanists might say that the love of neighbor is the *same* as the love of God, one will find in the social encyclicals an emphatic affirmation of the value of love of God as a way to *grow* in love of neighbor. Prayer and action are not mutually exclusive. As Saint Ignatius put it, we are to work as though everything depended upon us and pray as though everything depended on God. Secular humanist messages emphasize only the human responsibility side of this equation. Christians ought to remember that our God also has a stake in human history. If the future of planet Earth depends solely upon human effort, then there is little reason to hope. As history clearly reveals, we have demonstrated in countless distressing ways an almost complete inability to maintain peace and harmony among ourselves.

A second area in which Christian humanism needs balancing is in the realm of ethics. The classicist world view which supported the Church's Natural Law morality has been replaced by a world view that is less static and more historically conscious. But it does not follow from this shift in perspective that all of the old moral norms are now outdated. This matter of reinterpreting Christian moral norms is a complex task at which theologians have been hard at work in recent years. (See the Suggested Reading list on pages 125-126 for resources.) The most critical challenge, I believe, will be to counter the ethical relativity deriving from situation ethics. James Burtchaell, C.S.C., has made a significant contribution toward this end in his book *Philemon's Problem*.

A final concern for Christian humanists has to do with the manner in which we promote the Gospel. If it is true that the old forensic approach no longer works (although the fundamentalists are proving us wrong on this point), then we must be faithful to Christian tradition when formulating a new evangelical metaphor. I do not believe the clinical metaphor with its heavy emphasis on only the positive aspects of Christianity is entirely faithful to the Gospel. Although it is true that living the Christian life helps one to become more fully human, it should be noted that human fulfillment is but a *consequence* — and not the goal — of Christian living. The *goal* of a Christian is the faithful following of Jesus Christ — of bringing our will into conformity with his. In order to do so, however, we must first renounce our way, then pick up the Cross of dying to selfishness for the sake of love (Mark 8:34). The reason we must renounce our way is not simply because it is based on ignorance or erroneous zones of thinking, but because it is contemptuous of God and the things of God. This may seem a somewhat cynical view of human nature, but those who have come to see themselves as creatures before God know how selfish and fickle unredeemed human nature can be. The old forensic approach took all this into account; the new clinical evangelist speaks little about sinful human nature and even less about the Cross.

But it *is* true that secular humanism has led to the loss of a sense of sin in many, and it *is* equally true that the forensic appeal has lost its hold among the "guiltless." Clinical theologians have responded by attempting to make the Gospel more appealing, but I believe they have confused goals and consequences. We become fully human because we follow Jesus, and not vice versa. What is needed instead is a reinterpretation of sin, especially among these "guiltless" millions who *are* nonetheless sinners. Perhaps the two evangelical metaphors can complement each other in this most important of all endeavors. What follows is a suggested reformulation.

1. *All of us live in sin.* We hurt others; we turn our backs on those in need; we spend most of our time pondering ways to better our own lot and seldom think about how our plans fit into God's plan for us. Consequently, we do not live up to the best that is in us — the ideal self that we sense we can be. We hurt ourselves because of this falling short of the mark (which is a traditional definition of sin), and our relationships suffer as well. Selfish behaviors are the primary causes of our failure to become our best selves, so selfishness serves the power of sin. Since we are all selfish, we are all sinners.

2. *Left to our own knowledge and resources, we cannot become our best selves.* This is what secular humanists are unwilling to admit. But because we are spiritual as well as psychophysical beings, it is impossible for us to become our best selves without God's grace working in us. It is therefore appropriate that we utilize our freedom and intelligence to renounce our selfish ways and to seek God's will for us.

3. *God has intervened on our behalf, especially in the person of Jesus Christ.* The Good News is that God has not abandoned us to

live in the frustration of knowing that there is a best self in us that we can never realize. In Jesus Christ, God has revealed to us his values and has taught us the true meaning of love. Through the death and Resurrection of Jesus, the power of sin in our world has been broken. If that were not enough, God shares with us his own Spirit, that we might, in our own spirits, gain the energy and insight to live as we are capable of living.

4. *Those who would become followers of Jesus Christ and gain access to the power and meaning that he gives must first renounce their own way of life* — especially those ways rooted in selfishness. Becoming our best selves means first renouncing our worst selves. There must be a turning away before there can be a genuine turning toward. The clinical metaphor does not sufficiently stress this point.

5. *We come to know Jesus Christ and the new self he helps us to realize through faith.* But what is faith? At last we are ready to reflect on this virtue.

Reflection/Discussion

1. What do you believe to be the greatest good supported by secular humanists? What is the greatest evil resulting from it?
2. "It doesn't matter whether a person believes in God or not. What matters is that we love one another." How do you respond to this claim?
3. Do you believe there are moral norms for behavior rooted in the Gospel and in Nature? Give a few examples.
4. How has secular humanism affected Christian humanism? Do you believe these changes are for the better?
5. What are the strengths and weaknesses of the forensic and clinical metaphors of salvation?
6. What is the most important thing secular humanists can learn from Christians?

5

The Response of Faith

> Therefore, since we are justified by faith, we have peace with God through our Lord Jesus Christ. Through him we have obtained access to this grace in which we stand, and we rejoice in our hope of sharing the glory of God. More than that, we rejoice in our sufferings, knowing that suffering produces endurance, and endurance produces character, and character produces hope, and hope does not disappoint us, because God's love has been poured into our hearts through the Holy Spirit who has been given to us. (Romans 5:1-5)

In the previous four chapters, we have taken issue with human selfishness, scientific materialism, a faulty theodicy, and secular humanism. Our critique in each case was from the standpoint of faith, and we tried to show how these issues lead people away from faith in God. In contrast, this chapter will be more positive and less critical; we shall concern ourselves with the place of faith in human life and how one may come to grow in faith.

Faith means many things to many people. Like the word *love,* the word *faith* is used to describe several kinds of attitudes. Most often it is associated with belief in God, but frequently it will refer to nonreligious sentiments — as, for example, when we tell people we have faith in them and in their abilities.

Among certain scholars, faith is sometimes viewed as anti-intellectual, or as a substitute for thinking. Others consider faith and intellectual development to be mutually supportive. What is certain is that faith in God is possible for young and old, rich and poor, smart and dumb. Faith, as we shall see, is one of the most uniquely human of all phenomena.

Spirituality in an Emergent Universe

Before discussing religious faith, we need to identify the context in which faith takes place. Faith is oriented toward that higher dimension of reality whom we call God, so it will be helpful to reflect upon the human spirit. It is the spirit in each of us that longs for God and moves us to faith.

In Chapter 2 we spoke of hierarchies of reality: physical, chemical, biological, and psychological. For each of these levels, we made two important points. First, stability and complexity at each level allows the next higher one to emerge. Second, each level is a unique phenomenon that takes on a life of its own. Thus, the human mind develops only after brain development has become sufficiently complex. Thus, the life of the mind constitutes a new dimension of reality that transcends nerve impulse transmissions, hormone secretions, etc. Human beings exchange thoughts with each other in a manner analogous to the flow of molecules through a cell. Just as organic molecules are life to a cell, thoughts are life for a human mind. This is the point that holistic thinkers have been making for some time.

Secular humanists and scientific materialists are perfectly willing to agree to the hierarchical system sketched thus far. But they are unwilling to go any further. For them, psychological life represents the highest dimension of reality; the human mind stands at the pinnacle of evolution. It is at this point that religious thinkers must part company with these secularists, for it is our contention that there is yet another dimension of reality that transcends the psychological even while embracing it. Furthermore, we maintain that our awareness of this higher dimension of reality is rooted in the mind itself and is basic to our nature. This mental faculty that is sensitive to transcendence is the human spirit.

The spiritual faculty is difficult to characterize. Unlike those mental faculties that are concerned with sensate phenomena and the ways of this world, the spiritual is concerned with Ultimate Issues. As Karl Rahner puts it, "Even in its summing up, the ever finite thought of the human mind leaves intact that vastness to which spirit is open, and can never adequately correspond to the spirit's absolute and infinite expectancy." (*Dictionary of Theology*, Second Edition, page 486) Placing it in its hierarchical context, we might say that the spirit focuses mental activity toward a higher level of reality. It is the human spirit that leads us to organize thoughts into philosophies that we might understand the meaning of our lives. But, as Rahner has pointed out, human philosophy alone cannot fulfill the desires of the human spirit. Only God can quench this thirst. As Saint Augustine wrote, "Thou hast made us for thyself, O Lord, and our hearts will not rest until they rest in thee." The human spirit is God's image and likeness within us. We can deny its existence out of intellectual pride, but we cannot shake its demands upon our lives.

A human person represents the sum total of cosmic evolution. Our bodies were made possible through physical, chemical, and biological evolution. Mental life resides in our incredibly complex brains. And it is imperative now that we recognize a spiritual dimension to our nature. Indeed, spiritual growth represents our evolutionary future; failure to grow in this area will result in psychological stultification and a deeper entrenchment of the power of sin among us. Becoming a spiritually mature person is what faith makes possible, for faith establishes the link between the human spirit and the Spirit of God.

Before moving on, we need to recognize the sobering fact that it is possible for a person to so neglect and denigrate his or her spiritual needs as to become totally disinterested in faith. People who spend most of their time involved in selfish pursuits or in entertaining distractions such as television watching can lose their hunger for the things of God. I recall a letter I recently received from a friend. He told me that he had enjoyed reading my book *Becoming a New Person,* but he didn't understand it because he wasn't a religious person. My response to him was that he didn't understand it because he was spiritually numbed-out from years of spiritual neglect. (I am not usually so blunt and critical, but elsewhere in his letter he was chiding me.) This loss of spiritual interest is very common because modern culture does little to encourage and support spiritual pursuits as in decades past. Anyone who works with teenagers in CCD knows only too well how the lack of family and cultural support has allowed television, rock music, and alcohol to misdirect our young people's yearning for God.

Faith and Spiritual Development

"Now faith is the assurance of things hoped for, the conviction of things not seen," wrote the author of the Book of Hebrews (11:1). This most common definition of faith tells us several things:

1. Faith is oriented toward a higher dimension of reality, toward "things not seen." In the Letter to the Hebrews, as elsewhere in Scripture, this realm of the invisible includes God as well as finite spirits, including evil spirits.

2. Faith enables a connection between our own psychic processes and God. True faith is never anti-intellectual; true faith makes full use of reason, imagination, memory, feeling, and will.
3. Faith produces convictions that relate this life to a higher context. It is this perspective that enabled the critiques in Chapters 1 through 4.
4. Faith thus enables the formation of identity with respect to God. In addition to feedback from the human community, faith allows us to learn about ourselves in relation to God.
5. Faith is closely related to hope, which is also a spiritual virtue. A healthy spiritual life helps one to become hopeful, and faith brings assurance that what we hope for shall come to pass.

Faith in God is our most uniquely human quality. There is a story about two anthropologists who traveled back in time and came upon an ape-man roasting a piece of meat. Trying to determine if the ape-man was yet human, one of the anthropologists remarked, "Look, he cooks his food and uses tools: he must be human." The other anthropologist shook his head; he wasn't convinced. But when the ape-man paused to say a prayer before eating his meal, the second anthropologist said, "He's human, all right." I can think of no other more uniquely human characteristic than our capacity for religious faith. Every other human quality, including self-consciousness and language, can be found in some rudimentary degree in at least a few higher vertebrates.

The human capacity for religious faith is made possible because of our spiritual nature. But if it is true that the spirit makes faith possible, it is equally true that *faith enhances spiritual growth*. Spiritual growth is made possible because of faith, and this growth may begin in early childhood and continue until death. In his landmark work, *Stages of Faith: The Psychology of Human Development and the Quest for Meaning*, James Fowler has clearly described the relationship between faith and our more natural human growth patterns. Fowler describes in detail six stages of faith, which can be summarized briefly as follows:

1. *Childish faith*. Spiritual impulses derive from levels that are mostly unconscious and not yet integrated with one's identity. God is sensed as something greater; religious awe is felt most intensely. Because of a lack of intellectual development, belief in magic and superstitions is strong. Thomas Green, S.J., describes one's God-concept at this stage as that of a "puppeteer God" who pulls the strings which cause all of reality to dance. Both Fowler and Green maintain that many people carry vestiges of this kind of faith into adulthood.

2. *Adolescent faith*. The search for identity is most intense during the adolescent years. As one becomes self-conscious, reality takes on a more personal and intense meaning. These struggles are usually worked out in a context of peer interaction which, according to Fowler, is what characterizes adolescent faith. Adolescent faith is more personal than childish faith, but it is primarily mediated through a group. God is viewed as the guarantor of group norms. For example, if one's Christian group emphasizes patriotism, adolescent faith will be critical of any Christian group that minimizes the importance of patriotism in following Jesus Christ. "If you don't believe as we do, then you're wrong" is the stance of adolescent faith. Many adults cherish this adolescent "God of the group." Fowler maintains that it is the most commonly noted faith stage of all.

3. *Adult faith*. This stage is marked by a self-directed desire to conform one's identity and will to Christ's. Although group feedback is taken into consideration, belief is less dependent on group norms and more centered in one's perceptions of God's

will. At this adult level of faith, a person has a sense of being a co-redeemer of the world with Christ. This sense of shared responsibility is different from allegiance to a human authority figure; the authority here is God, and adult faith readily submits to his will. Thomas H. Green, S.J., describes this God-concept as that of the "Father of adult children." Submission to God is therefore an act of loving and informed obedience rather than a peer-pressure response as in adolescent faith or a fear-response as in childish faith.

Taking a cue from biology, we might find these faith-stage descriptions helpful in viewing human spiritual development from an historical viewpoint. Biologists often look to individual development for clues concerning evolutionary development. They have a saying — "Ontology recapitulates phylogeny" — which means that the stages we see in individual development are the same stages we can expect in the evolution of the human species. History shows many cases of cultures with childish faith. Various primitive cultures, for example, still practice magical rites and worship more than one god. Another example is the adolescent faith of early Judaism with its strong emphasis on tribalism, covenant, and law. Adolescent faith may also be found among Christian denominations which hold that their way is the only right way to God.

In contrast, adult faith marked the Jewish prophets and the mystics of all religions. Adult faith is especially encouraged by Jesus, the Son of God, who calls each of us to follow him in our own uniqueness as we hear his voice in our lives (see John 10:3).

Faith is rooted in the human hunger for God. It grows through time, paralleling and complementing our growth in identity and knowledge. Faith forms our thoughts, directs our lives, and fills our minds with meaning.

But how does one "get" such faith?

Developing Faith Convictions

Our spiritual longing is a natural and uniquely human part of our nature. It usually manifests itself in the search for meaning, or, more specifically, in the many kinds of pursuits wherein we try to complete ourselves. Food, money, alcohol, romantic love, status, and friendships all bring temporary gratification to our spiritual needs. But then these pursuits leave us hungering for more. How often do we read about a person who had everything, and then committed suicide! As Qoheleth so honestly put it in the Book of Ecclesiastes, all human success and striving leaves one, at the end of it all, feeling empty and incomplete. (Read chapters 1 through 3 of Ecclesiastes.)

The human spirit's true home is with God, and to be truly human means to root one's life in God. But God cannot be found as one finds, say, a better job. Despite the immensity of its longing, the human spirit cannot reach out to the heavens and embrace God. Any contact with God that we may experience depends upon God's initiative. God, if he is to be found, must reveal himself to us. Unless God does so, we shall perceive only his reflections in our own spirit and in creation. When we speak of faith as the bridge between the human spirit and God, we must acknowledge the fact that God is the one who builds this bridge. This is why the Church speaks of faith as a gift; it is a virtue that we do not earn nor even deserve. The most that we can do is to ask and seek and knock on the doors of heaven, knowing all the while that it is God's will that we come to know him through faith (Matthew 7:7-11).

In Hebrews 11:1, we read that faith is a "conviction of things not seen," divine things. *Conviction* is a strong word. In this context it implies the state of being utterly convinced of God's real presence in our lives. This assurance concerning our relationship with God makes possible the development of a new identity. Saint Paul and other New Testament writers seem to take for granted that

God wants us to develop such intense faith convictions that we are filled with confidence concerning God's will for us. Far from viewing faith as an extraordinary state of mind or a rare and unusual phenomenon, the early Church maintained that faith in Jesus Christ represents the most authentic stance that a human being can take in this world. (See Romans 5:2; 1 Corinthians 16:3; 2 Corinthians 5:7; Galatians 2:20; Ephesians 3:12.)

Growing in our faith convictions represents one of our greatest human challenges. Fortunately, the Scriptures and the writings of saints through the centuries provide guidelines about how we come to know God through faith and how we grow in faith. The following is a description of the steps people go through in receiving the gift of faith:

1. *We recognize the folly of trying to fulfill ourselves through selfish pursuits and behaviors.* We know this through the hopelessness and sense of guilt that our ways leave untouched within us.

2. *We believe that God wants us to know him.* Christ stands at the door of the human spirit and knocks, ready to come in and live with us, but waiting patiently for our invitation (Revelation 3-20).

3. *We ask God to forgive us and to make his home within us.* We plead that his Spirit will form our own spirits in his ways (see 1 Corinthians 2:10-16).

Ideally, it is in the context of family or community that one becomes predisposed to accept this greatest of all gifts. God's forgiveness and invitation come to us through the Word of God proclaimed and lived out in community. Faith comes through hearing the Word of God (Romans 10:17), but this Word is mediated through people. It is the community of faith called the Church which now extends the invitation to relationship with God that Jesus once revealed so unambiguously. Unfortunately, many people do not enjoy the kind of Christian family living or community involvement that nurtures faith. That is why those of us who have come to know God through faith must take seriously our "splendid burden of working to make the divine message of salvation known and accepted by all men throughout the world" (*The Documents of Vatican II*, Decree on the Laity, 3). We are all called to Christian discipleship.

After an individual asks God for the gift of faith, he or she may rest assured that the gift has been given. I have known people who experienced in their first serious request for faith a dramatic and illuminating experience of God. These fortunate few (I am convinced that they are a minority) have little difficulty in developing convictions about God's presence in their lives. Faith, for them, begins with a bang; only later do they settle into a pattern of slow and gradual spiritual growth. For most of us, the beginning of faith is not dramatic. A small seed of faith is planted in whatever good soil may be found in our hearts. Then it grows by being watered and cared for daily.

Growth in faith requires from us an ongoing regimen of spiritual reading, prayer, involvement in community, and an attempt to lead a life of love. If we fall short in any of these four areas, we can expect to suffer consequences in our growth in Christ. Let us briefly acknowledge the role of each in our spiritual growth.

1. *Spiritual reading* helps the mind become resistant to the world's invitations to attain spiritual gratification through selfish means. Reading also introduces us to the wisdom of others who have traveled the path of faith. It enables us to learn from them. Finally, spiritual books help us to employ our mental faculties toward their proper end: the knowledge of God and his will for us.

2. *Prayer.* Every time people have come to me complaining that they have no sense of God's presence in their lives, it has always been the case that they had stopped praying. In our human relationships we do not get to know others unless we take time to dialogue with them. Why should we expect it to be any different with God? Anyone serious about growing in faith should be committed to at least one period of quiet time with God each day. This time should be spent mostly in silent and loving attentiveness, especially to the word God speaks to us in Scripture.

3. *Community involvement.* The individual Christian is but one cell in the Body of Christ, his Church. We need to be open to the grace that God extends to us through other Christians. Their gifts complement ours; their strengths support us in our weaknesses.

4. *Lifestyle.* Living a life of faith means becoming a disciple of Christ. Faith enables us to live a life of love in a world that all too often shows itself to be callous and resistant to the ways of love. But living a life of love also enables us to grow in faith, for in our struggle to love we discover the relationship between faith and the Cross. There can be no true Christian faith without the Cross of Jesus Christ. Learning to carry our own crosses is a key to spiritual growth.

Faith and the Cross

Faith establishes connections between the human spirit and God. God does, of course, influence the lives of people who do not consciously seek relationship with him. Christ, as we know, is the source of all that is human in everyone who has ever lived (Acts 17:28; James 1:17). But people of faith have made a decision to *welcome* God's influence, a decision to become more open and receptive to being motivated by the Spirit of God. So we can expect to find God's love more consistently manifest in the lives of people of faith. Real faith — that is, faith that really connects us with God — can be expected to produce loving results in our lives, for God is love (1 John 4:7). Jesus did not intend us to believe in God just for the sake of belief. As Saint James reminds us, even the devil believes in God (James 2:19). Jesus commanded us to *love* God (Mark 12:39).

The problem that people of faith always encounter is that the world often seems callous and even hostile toward the ways of love. This resistance is partly rooted in our unwillingness to change. Love accepts people as they are, but it implicitly denounces all human selfishness. Breaking out of selfish habits can be a very painful growth process, and we would rather not experience the suffering that always accompanies growth. This explains, in part, the ill treatment to which the great lovers in history are subjected. But there is more to it than that.

Scripture and tradition teach us that God's love arouses hostility in many because it is totally incompatible with Evil Spirit. Faith makes us members of God's Kingdom, but there is another kingdom fighting desperately for control of the earth. "For we are not contending against flesh and blood, but against the principalities, against the powers, against the world rulers of this present darkness, against the spiritual hosts of wickedness in the heavenly places." (Ephesians 6:12) There is a spiritual adversary who is diametrically opposed to God and his designs. This spirit is Lucifer, a fallen angel, whose army of followers still works to tempt us away from God by distorting everything that is good and holy.

We have mentioned the influence of Evil Spirit elsewhere in this book, for the Church teaches quite clearly that Satan is not merely a symbolic personalizing of human evil. I believe it is imperative that we take seriously the existence of Evil Spirit in order to comprehend the true meaning of the Gospel. But as we also mentioned earlier (especially in Chapter 4), it has become trendy to interpret the coming of Christ solely as a gift to enhance humanization. Such a completely humanistic emphasis ignores the many references to the Cross as the tool by which Jesus overthrew the Prince of this World (see John 12:31, 14:30, 16:11; 1 John 3:8). It was through his death and Resurrection that Jesus broke the viselike grip that Satan had on this world, making it possible now for the Spirit of God to leaven a more human world for all of us. But Christ's victory only established the *potential* for the reign of God; its *actuality* must be won through the Church in time. Meanwhile, although it has been in retreat since the Resurrection of Jesus, the kingdom of Satan still influences many of our earthly affairs. That kingdom will not be fully eradicated until the Second Coming.

I believe our naïveté concerning the ultimate source of human evil is a very great danger. As Malachi Martin wrote in his book *Hostage to the Devil,* "No one wants to believe in evil, really, above all, not in an evil being, an evil spirit. Everyone wants to abolish the idea. To admit the existence of evil means a responsibility, and no one wants *that* responsibility." Perhaps the following exchange, quoted in *Hostage to the Devil,* can help to awaken us to the kinds of forces against which Christian love must do battle.

Before expelling a demon, the exorcist must interview it briefly to learn the extent of its possession of a soul. Only then can it be totally uprooted. After questioning the demon at some length, the exorcist in the situation we are considering asked:

"Why did you lead Carl in this way?"
"Because he would lead others."
"Lead others in what way?"
"Because then they belong to the Kingdom."
"Why belong to the Kingdom?"

" . . . *Why,* Priest? *Why?* You stand there with your bald head, your scorched testicles, your smelly clothes, your yellowing teeth, your stinking guts, and you ask us *why? Why? Why? Why? Why?*" The word comes out on the crest of ever-louder shouts.

"*WHY?*" he finally shouts at the top of his voice, his head raised to stare at Hearty (the Priest). "*Why?* Because we hate the Latter (Christ). We hate. Hate. Hate. We hate those stained with his blood. We hate and despise those that follow him. We want to divert all from him and we want all in the Kingdom where he cannot reach them. Where they cannot go with him. And we want you, Priest! Because we have Carl. He is ours. And no power can undo our hold on him. No power. No power!"

Christian lovers can expect to encounter resistances that will test faith to the extreme. (Incidentally, Carl, in the above-mentioned case, was eventually cleansed.)

The Cross means persevering in love even in the face of overwhelming evil. It means suffering through whatever obstacles and temptations may come our way, holding fast only to the power of God while striving to discern his will. Satan will do everything possible to discourage us and lead us away from God. Secular humanism, distorted theodicy, scientific materialism, and consumerism are snares commonly used in this day and age. But the Cross teaches us that we must be willing to trust in God even when the world, the flesh, and the devil would lead us to believe that God's way is utter nonsense, or even harmful.

Still, we must carefully discern when we are called to perfect our faith through suffering love. The Christian, like Christ, must learn when it is appropriate to do fierce battle with evil and how this battle shall take place. Jesus avoided a decisive confrontation with evil many times (John 2:4; Luke 4:30). When his hour finally arrived, it would have been too easy for him to run from it, maintaining that he could better further God's Kingdom by preaching and healing as he had been. We, too, are often called to do battle with evil for the sake of love, advancing God's reign while keeping Satan in retreat. But we must pick our battles carefully; we must carry our crosses only when life and the Kingdom of love truly require this of us. If we learn to do so, we will discover, like Jesus, that the Cross opens the door to assurance concerning God's providence in our lives.

Life in the Spirit

Faith introduces us to a kind of knowledge that human intelligence alone cannot attain. God's message to us might be summed up quite simply as: "I love you. Will you let me love you that you may learn to love?" When other people tell us "I love you," we encounter the same invitation. We can look for signs of the reality of their love, but we cannot prove that they love us as we can demonstrate that two plus two equals four. The only way to know their love is to enter into it — to open ourselves to being touched by them. This involves trust, for a certain element of control must be given up when we accept another's love. But such acceptance leads to a new kind of knowledge — love knowledge — and immerses us in a level of reality that reason alone cannot comprehend. This is how it is with God. Faith enables us to receive his love, which in turn imparts within us a new understanding of love and life.

Many preachers like to make a distinction between coming to Christ through faith and accepting the gift of the Holy Spirit. Although their theology is often atrocious (as though one could believe in Christ and not be moved by the Spirit!) the reality they describe is quite accurate. Faith makes it possible for us to know God in a new way, but living by the power of the Holy Spirit involves a deeper level of commitment. It means relinquishing control of our lives to the control of the Spirit. I believe that many good people of faith have yet to experience the Spirit in this manner.

The New Testament often alludes to baptism of water *and* the Spirit (John 3:5; Titus 3:5). After people came to believe the Good News and became members of the Church through Baptism, the apostles were called upon to lay hands on them that they might be renewed also in the Holy Spirit. In Acts 8:14-17, for example, we read:

> Now when the apostles at Jerusalem heard that Samaria had received the word of God, they sent to them Peter and John, who came down and prayed for them that they might receive the Holy Spirit; for it had not yet fallen on any of them, but they had only been baptized in the name of the Lord Jesus. Then they laid their hands on them and they received the Holy Spirit.

This is why the Church came to celebrate both Baptism and Confirmation as two different sacraments of faith. Confirmation enables us to grow beyond childish and adolescent levels of faith, becoming a people who know themselves to be adult children of God.

Mature, adult Christians are called not only to believe in Christ but also to live by the power of his Spirit. Because the powers of evil against which we struggle are so much greater than mere human intelligence and willpower, we need the power of the Holy Spirit to help us persevere in love. Satan is a preternatural spirit, whose powers are immensely greater than our human spiritual powers (although Satan cannot violate the integrity of the human will but must depend upon its cooperation); God is a supernatural Spirit, whose authority and power is immeasurably greater than Satan's. Because of the gift of the Holy Spirit, we may rejoice, therefore, that there is one in us who is greater than the one who is of the world (1 John 4:4). But in order to appreciate this assurance, we must allow the Holy Spirit to work within us.

It is unfortunate that so many Christians have come to associate the invitation to a baptism in the Holy Spirit with pentecostal or charismatic groups. While it is certain that these groups whole-heartedly welcome the baptism in the Spirit, there can be no doubt that the Holy Spirit is ready and willing to renew people who are not members of a pentecostal community. A pentecostal group can help one to become more open to the Holy Spirit. Such groups provide the teaching, prayer, openness, and enthusiasm for the gifts of the Spirit that help an individual to become open and receptive. But any Christian who asks for assistance from the Holy Spirit for living a life of love may be assured that the Spirit will be given (Luke 11:9-13). This gift may be received through prayer or reception of the Eucharist, as well as through the mediation of a pentecostal group.

Baptism in the Holy Spirit enables us to become intimate friends with God. Intimacy, by definition, means "belonging to or charac-terizing one's deepest nature." Just as the human spirit lies at the heart and core of our identity, so too does the Holy Spirit proceed from the heart of God. Therefore, "we have received not the spirit of the world, but the Spirit which is from God, that we might understand the gifts bestowed on us by God" (1 Corinthians 2:12). The Holy Spirit is God's very life living within us, helping us to become a new person, a spiritual person — a fully human person. "For all who are led by the Spirit of God are sons of God . . . the Spirit himself bearing witness with our spirit that we are children of God." (Romans 8:14,16) The Spirit enables us to know God intimately, to call God *Abba,* or Daddy (Romans 8:15).

People who do not enjoy the fullness of the Spirit that Christ won for us are very likely to identify themselves with their bodily and psychological needs. But the Holy Spirit enables our natural faculties of body and mind to become focused in Christ. This does not mean that we lose our individuality or judgment, however. On the contrary, those who live by the Spirit know themselves as children of God, which is an infinitely more stable self-concept than looking to the world for reflections of selfhood. And because the Spirit enables us to see things from God's perspective instead of through our own twisted self-interest, our faculties of judgment are freed to recognize new alternatives and to choose wisely. The Holy Spirit deepens identity and helps us to become more decisive and more responsible.

It should be noted, however, that this heightened sense of identity and freedom do not mean that we enjoy perfect identification with Christ and perfect knowledge of his will. With Saint Paul, we must admit that our vision is often foggy, that ''now we see in a mirror dimly, but then face to face'' (1 Corinthians 13:12). With the exception of Jesus, spiritual perfection has never been attained in this world. All of us must continually struggle to identify ourselves with the spiritual rather than the psychological (as secular humanism would have it) or merely physical (as scientific materialism and consumerism propose). Only at the resurrection of the dead will we be fully clothed in the spiritual glory that is our true inheritance. ''If the Spirit of him who raised Jesus from the dead dwells in you, he who raised Christ Jesus from the dead will give life to your mortal bodies also through his Spirit who dwells in you.'' (Romans 8:11)

Gone is the medieval Church, with its primary emphasis upon life's purpose as the salvation of one's soul. Yet, I hope that in expanding on this central focus we have not lost it. For the truth remains that our eternal destiny lies with either God or Satan. Life is serious business, and the stakes are of eternal importance to the individual. I hope that what we are trying to do through education and social action is to create a human society that better facilitates and supports the individual in her or his journey to God. If we are attempting to build the earthly city for our own enjoyment only, and without regard for the ways of God, then Satan will reap a harvest of millions of souls in the process. But if we persist in living a life of love through faith and the power of the Holy Spirit, then we shall find "the sufferings of this present time are not worth comparing with the glory that is to be revealed to us." (Romans 8:18) Then, too, will the world as a whole draw closer to God and the coming of his Kingdom among us, for the salvation of an individual soul improves the well-being of the entire cosmos (Luke 15:10).

Reflection/Discussion

1. What does faith mean to you?
2. How do you experience the Cross in your life of faith?
3. Do you believe faith is compatible with reason? Explain.
4. What does baptism in the Holy Spirit mean to you?
5. Which of the sources of doubt discussed in the book causes you the most difficulty? Why?

Suggested Reading

Chapter One: The Challenge of Selfishness

Russell M. Abata, C.SS.R., S.T.D., *How to Develop a Better Self-Image,* Liguori Publications, 1980.

Ralph F. Ranieri, *Christian Living: Ten Basic Virtues,* Liguori Publications, 1983.

Edward Richardson, M.M., *Love Yourself,* Liguori Publications, 1970.

Fulton J. Sheen, *Lift Up Your Heart,* Doubleday Image Books, 1951.

Philip St. Romain, *Becoming a New Person: Twelve Steps to Christian Growth,* Liguori Publications, 1984.

Chapter Two: The Challenge of Scientific Materialism

Pierre Teilhard de Chardin, *Christianity and Evolution,* Harcourt Brace Jovanovich, 1974.

John F. Haught, *The Cosmic Adventure,* Paulist Press, 1984.

Chapter Three: The Challenge of Suffering and Evil

Harold S. Kushner, *When Bad Things Happen to Good People,* Avon Books, 1981.

C. S. Lewis, *The Problem of Pain,* Macmillan Publishing Company, 1978.

M. Scott Peck, M.D., *The Road Less Traveled,* Simon & Schuster, 1978.

M. Scott Peck, M.D., *People of the Lie,* Simon & Schuster, 1983.

Chapter Four: The Challenge of Secular Humanism

James T. Burtchaell, C.S.C., *Philemon's Problem: The Daily Dilemma of the Christian,* ACTA Foundation, 1973.

Richard M. Gula, S.S., *What Are They Saying About Moral Norms?,* Paulist Press, 1982.

James Hitchcock, *What Is Secular Humanism?,* Servant Books, 1982.

Xavier Thevenot, *Sin: A Christian View for Today,* Liguori Publications, 1984.

Chapter Five: The Response of Faith

James W. Fowler, *Stages of Faith: The Psychology of Human Development and the Quest for Meaning,* Harper & Row, 1981.

Teofilio Cabestrero, ed., *Faith: Conversations with Contemporary Theologians,* Orbis Books, 1980.

MORE HELPFUL BOOKS
FROM PHILIP ST. ROMAIN

BECOMING A NEW PERSON
Twelve Steps to Christian Growth

Based on the world-famous Twelve Steps, this easy-to-understand program can help any adult Christian embark on a new, freer way of life. $2.95

HOW TO FORM
A CHRISTIAN GROWTH SUPPORT GROUP

A manual to accompany the popular *Becoming a New Person,* these pages explain what a CG group is, how to organize one, and what takes place at group meetings. It makes the Twelve Steps a practical plan for any group whose goal is spiritual growth. $2.95

CATHOLIC ANSWERS
TO FUNDAMENTALISTS' QUESTIONS

This book, written for Catholics, as well as questioning Fundamentalists, offers clear, accurate answers to a great many questions that sincere Christians ask about the Catholic Church. $1.50

Order from your local bookstore or write to:
Liguori Publications, Box 060, Liguori, Missouri 63057
*(Please add 50¢ for postage and handling for first
item ordered and 25¢ for each additional item.)*